ASIA-PACIFIC
DEVELOPMENT
JOURNAL

Vol. 16, No. 2, December 2009

United Nations
New York, 2010

ECONOMIC AND SOCIAL COMMISSION FOR ASIA AND THE PACIFIC

ASIA-PACIFIC DEVELOPMENT JOURNAL

Vol. 16, No.2, December 2009

United Nations publication
Sales No. E.09.II.F.20
Copyright © United Nations 2010
All rights reserved
Manufactured in Thailand
ISBN: 978-92-1-120587-9
ISSN: 1020-1246
ST/ESCAP/2548

Advisory Board

Editorial statement

The *Asia-Pacific Development Journal* is published twice a year by the Economic and Social Commission for Asia and the Pacific.

Its primary objective is to provide a medium for the exchange of knowledge, experience, ideas, information and data on all aspects of economic and social development in the Asian and Pacific region. The emphasis of the *Journal* is on the publication of empirically based, policy-oriented articles of broad socio-economic development issues.

The *Journal* welcomes original articles analysing issues and problems relevant to the region from the above perspective. The articles should have a strong emphasis on the policy implications flowing from the analysis. Analytical book reviews will also be considered for publication.

Manuscripts should be sent to:

Chief Editor
Asia-Pacific Development Journal
Macroeconomic Policy and Development Division
ESCAP, United Nations Building
Rajadamnern Nok Avenue
Bangkok 10200
Thailand
Fax: (662) 288-3007 or (662) 288-1000
Email:escap-mpdd@un.org

ASIA-PACIFIC DEVELOPMENT JOURNAL
Vol. 16, No. 2, December 2009

CONTENTS

Explanatory notes

References to dollars ($) are to United States dollars, unless otherwise stated.

References to "tons" are to metric tons, unless otherwise specified.

A solidus (/) between dates (e.g. 1980/81) indicates a financial year, a crop year or an academic year.

Use of a hyphen between dates (e.g. 1980-1985) indicates the full period involved, including the beginning and end years.

The following symbols have been used in the tables throughout the *Journal*:

An em-dash (—) indicates that the amount is nil or negligible.

A hyphen (-) indicates that the item is not applicable.

A point (.) is used to indicate decimals.

A space is used to distinguish thousands and millions.

Totals may not add precisely because of rounding.

The designations employed and the presentation of the material in this publication do not imply the expression of any opinion whatsoever on the part of the Secretariat of the United Nations concerning the legal status of any country, territory, city or area or of its authorities, or concerning the delimitation of its frontiers or boundaries.

Where the designation "country or area" appears, it covers countries, territories, cities or areas.

Bibliographical and other references have, wherever possible, been verified. The United Nations bears no responsibility for the availability or functioning of URLs.

The opinions, figures and estimates set forth in this publication are the responsibility of the authors, and should not necessarily be considered as reflecting the views or carrying the endorsement of the United Nations. Mention of firm names and commercial products does not imply the endorsement of the United Nations.

ON STRUCTURED BUYER-SELLER NEGOTIATION FOR AGRICULTURAL LAND ACQUISITION - SIMULATION EXPERIMENTS WITH RULE-BASED MODELS AND UTILITY FUNCTIONS

Usha Sridhar and Sridhar Mandyam*

The acquisition of land from landowning communities for the purpose of expanding industry has been a part of economic strategy in many developing countries in the past decade. The lack of a structured negotiation framework to ensure equity and transparency in the process of acquisition has been an important issue in many of these countries, particularly India. Among the core issues are the lack of a well defined process framework, authorized regulatory and statutory entities to participate and oversee the process, and transparent mechanisms for calculating and communicating offers and valuations between the buyer and the seller communities. There is a need to explore alternative negotiation frameworks and models for calculation and valuation of bids and asks which can ensure an adequate level of equity and transparency. The models must ensure that the compensation packages cover certain basic needs of the small and medium farmers for whom loss of land is also loss of livelihood.

In this paper, we propose a framework for land acquisition negotiations in which mathematical models for the buyer generate price offers not only for land but also wage and other compensations. We also present utility-based models and a rule base for the seller to evaluate the offer, and mechanisms for the seller's responses to be communicated via intermediaries to the buyer in cycles of negotiation. Using simulated data representative of the agricultural land scenario in India, we explore ways in which the models and the framework could be used to support diverse and realistic land acquisition situations. Software for the implementation of the mathematical models and rule engine for evaluation of the bid-ask process described in this paper have been developed by the authors. The software can be customized for specific applications.

I. INTRODUCTION

In recent years, several large-scale land acquisition attempts for the purpose of expanding India's industrial footprint have been stuck in the quagmire of controversy. There has been both public outcry and serious published critiques (Sangvai 2006, Basu 2007, Chandra 2008, Sau 2008, Gupta 2008, Sanhati 2008, Banerjee et al 2007, Morris and Pandey 2007) that point to important lacunae in the process of land acquisition. There is also a raging debate on an array of legal and socio-economic development issues that

* The authors are co-founders of Ecometrix Research. The present paper is an updated and revised version of an internal unpublished technical paper developed as part of the research activity at the organization. The authors would like to thank the anonymous referees for helpful comments on an earlier draft.

seem to stand in the way of individual corporate efforts at the state level to acquire large parcels of land for industry. It is estimated that an investment of over $600 billion for about 200 proposed special economic zones (SEZs), many of which would require at least 1,000 hectares of land across India, has been held up due to land acquisition issues. It also appears that a complex combination of competitive pressures to draw large-scale private investment to state hinterlands in the hope of enhancing employment prospects often conflicts with the needs of industry to locate itself in close proximity to available resources of industrial/ transportation infrastructure and labour. This very often places selected locations squarely in the midst of agricultural land rather than wasteland.

The result is that buyers have sought to acquire agricultural land from communities of farmers. Despite a few success stories, many efforts have largely been ineffectual, often leaving the potential selling community seeking aggressive, sometimes violent means to stave off what they consider "forced" acquisition attempt at highly "unreasonable" prices (Debroy 2008, Datta 2008, Das 2007). The situation has naturally been worse in cases where the large land parcel sought is highly fragmented with a larger proportion of marginal and small farmers, for whom loss of land is also equivalent to loss of livelihood. Valuation and pricing of such land is evidently a tricky trade-off, for it can impact not only the farming community but also the very financial viability of the industry whose presence and eventual growth is expected to lift substantial proportions of the farming community, especially small and marginal farmers, out of a potentially unsustainable income de-growth cycle (Bhaduri 2007). The problem is further exacerbated in regions where large populations continue to live off the land without proper titles, and when quasi-legal categories of rights are created by local governments for such communities (such as West Bengal, India).

At the core of the problem are a number of socio-economic, community development, legal and process issues that do not seem to address the concerns of the seller community.

The central concerns that have been articulated in current literature are:

(a)   The legal framework is archaic and does not adequately secure the position of the sellers, even in the newly amended draft Act (India 2007a, India 2007b);

(b)   Rates per hectare of agricultural land are not arrived at by negotiations in a scientific and transparent manner, but fixed using rather arbitrary and ad hoc mechanisms;

(c)   The net compensations for marginal and small farmers do not adequately ameliorate their social standing through the provision of opportunities for alternative livelihood and/or sources of secure future income, rather they take away their only source of current income, however meagre;

(d)   The process of acquisition often lacks transparency, the larger issue being the lack of a regulatory and ombudsman framework which can guide the process in the interest of equity and fairness to both buyers and sellers.

Many of the above issues have defied easy solutions. There have been reports of several debates on the legal aspects of how "public purpose" has come to mean "forced" acquisition (Basu 2007, Sau 2008). In this paper, however, we shall not concern ourselves with any of these legal aspects of land acquisition. Interestingly, in comparison with several other countries (Alias and Daud 2007), there is no mention of a *required* "negotiation" process for acquisition of land between buyers and sellers even in the new draft laws under consideration in India. Nevertheless, informal exchanges of bids and asks between the buyer, middlemen, and prospective sellers that have been followed in a majority of cases in India have, we believe, been one of the primary sources of conflict and confusion (Das 2006, Sanhati 2008). A structured negotiation framework is hence a key requirement for addressing this issue.

The "market" rate for agricultural land has defied a "standardized" index because of several factors, not the least of which is a transparent and honest registration process. As has been pointed out (Vijapurkar 2007b), averages over past years taken from neighbouring areas do not offer the benefit of a prospective growth to the seller. Other issues in this sphere point to a "speculative hold-out" by some sellers, which gives them an unfair bargaining position, while of course delaying closure of the negotiation (Bhaduri 2007). Most current proposals utilize some variation of a "guidance value" modulated by a "solatium" as a starting point. Equally, little has been said on a sound mechanism for sellers to evaluate an offer.

Our focus here is primarily on the mechanics of negotiation and on how to ensure transparency and equity in a process, which mandates that components of compensation be provided in order to protect the interests of the marginal and small farmer. While the data and context for the description of the problem have been taken to represent India in particular, we believe the overall solution approach may well be applicable to many other developing economies.

In this paper, we shall explore the possibility of building a structured approach to address the last two of the above concerns. Specifically, we propose a process by which the buyer and a group of potential sellers can arrive at a conclusive package of compensation for land through cycles of exchange of information capturing aggregate rates for compensation components. Our proposed process of negotiation requires that individual choice on the levels of compensation for each seller be collated and communicated to the buyer in such a manner as to avoid compromising the buy-sell posture of either economic agent while offering a degree of transparency through the definition of a scale-based response at the individual level. This exchange calls for intermediaries with specific roles, such as for financial intermediaries, potential government regulatory bodies or ombudsman bodies, and village-level or non-governmental organization (NGO) bodies. Within this structured framework for information exchange, we consider buyers and sellers as individual economic agents that evaluate compensation packages in accordance with the achievement of economic utility.

In order to explore the decision space in a quantifiable manner, we shall build mathematical models for the offers that the buyer can make, and similarly for the individual sellers to evaluate in terms of their own utility functions. We explore the possibility of a lexicographically ordered scale as the means to convey seller positions, so that the buyer can rework offers to begin subsequent negotiation cycles. We have also proposed overall measures to evaluate the impact of the transaction in terms of costs and benefit at the individual as well as community levels.

The models have been tested through simulation using two data sets representing a fictitious buyer and groups of sellers, whose overall demographic and landowning characteristics have been closely matched to real distributions of land owning patterns in rural India. The results of the application of the framework, buyer and seller models on the data are analysed to evaluate the utility of the concepts herein. Software for implementation of the mathematical models and rule engine for evaluation of the bid-ask process described in this paper have been developed by the authors. The software can be customized for specific applications.

The organization of the paper is as follows. The next section (section II) presents the buyer's offer model and the seller's valuation model, together with considerations for a framework in which the "bid" and "ask" information could be exchanged to meet the goal of allowing the process to be monitored by a small set of entities, which ensures the integrity of information and fair-play in the transactions. A description of the data generated for the purpose of simulating cycles of negotiation between a buyer and the sellers appears in section III. Section IV summarizes the overall mechanism proposed for initiating and running negotiation cycles, and offers roles and tasks for specific entities that have been proposed. Results of the simulation exercise are presented in section V, and discussions and concluding remarks appear in section VI.

II. APPROACH

The setting for the decision problem is thought to comprise one prospective buyer who wishes to acquire M hectares of agricultural land owned by N members of a farming community. All M hectares are assumed to be contiguous. The N members are thought to map onto N families for simplicity, although it is quite possible that more than one member of a family might legally own one or more parcels of land. The majority of the N potential sellers are thought to belong to, at most, a small number of communities within the same geographical region.

The land acquisition process is seen here essentially as two coupled decision problems, one, for the buyer, and the other a set of seller decision sub-problems. The information exchanged between these coupled problems forms the substrate for the negotiation process, with each party evaluating the current offer and articulating prospective action. As part of the preparatory process, we shall postulate at this stage the presence of an overseer entity (OE) that regulates the flow of this information between the buyer and the seller, maintaining the integrity of the information, and recording the changes for each side.

We shall first set preconditions for the process. One precondition is that the buyer shall be required to offer the overall compensation in the form of aggregate (meaning not on a per seller basis) offers for three components: (a) an aggregate sum towards immediate compensation for land alone; (b) an aggregate phased payment towards wage and other compensations; and (c) an aggregate sum set apart for the social development of the selling community as a whole. In a typical scenario, the buyer would be required to set up an initial budget and allocate proportions of it for the three components; zero proportions shall not be allowed. In order to pursue the negotiation, the buyer will require certain basic information on the status of the M hectares, the N sellers, and their current holdings distribution and demographics. Such information shall be assumed to be available from the above OE – another precondition. The buyer shall thus disclose to OE sums as described in (a) through (c) above. The OE shall be tasked to break down the sums as net subpart compensations for each seller on the basis of individual utilities. These break-ups shall not be disclosed to the buyer.

Some further explanation of this precondition is in order. Let us start with the price of land. As is well known, the price of a hectare of agricultural land intended for agricultural use is really related to a variety of factors, such as fertility, cropping pattern, potential income, crop yield, availability of storage barn, wells and trees. It is fair to assume that, in a transaction between agriculturists, the buyer and the seller would arrive at the price per hectare by using a combination of experience, knowledge of local conditions and the known history of such transactions in the same geographical area. However, in a situation where the intent is to use the land for industrial purposes, the experience and history can only be used to calculate wages and income, not to determine the primary land price. Hence, the buyer proceeds with negotiations using only a base-line land price, referenced by a notional "market" price. Seller-level assessment of land compensation is driven by individual perceptions. We are now ready to consider a schematic flow for the negotiations, as depicted in figure 1.

Figure 1. Initial schema for negotiations between buyer and seller

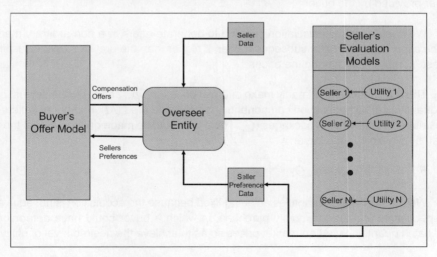

We shall see that the above schema can be expanded with the introduction of other entities as we refine the process further. For now, we are ready to explore the buyer and seller valuation models.

Buyer Model

The buyer is not expected to deal directly with individual sellers, but make offers to the OE, using publicly available data on the land holdings covering M hectares. Hence, the buyer can approach the decision problem purely from the perspective of minimizing outflow while obtaining the best possible trade-off between prices or rates paid for the three components of the compensation package. To quantify this trade-off, let us first define three prices.

Let p_1 denote the gross rate per hectare for land, p_2 denote net additional compensation per seller, and p_3 denote net rate per package offered for community development. Note that while p_1 is related purely to land, p_2 is a composite rate per seller comprising compensation for wages lost due to the sale of his land. A buyer could consider offering annual compensation, for instance, for 75 per cent of a year at rates varying from $1.60 a day to a buyer-chosen upper limit. The third rate, p_3, represents a per-package cost for social/ community development packages, broadly classifiable as a rehabilitation package. At the buyer end, we assume, these gross rates are sufficient to construct a gross compensation offer. In practice, it is indeed rare to find an industrial buyer attempting to delve down to the finer details in order to arrive at social and community development package prices.

The central theme around which the mechanics of a buyer model are built is to generate offers that fall within a budget for consideration by sellers. The upper limit of the budget will usually be set by a buyer on the basis of a variety of factors, most of which have to do with the alternative industrial use that the buyer will put the land to. How that should be done is clearly outside the scope of the negotiation process. We must simply accept the number provided by the buyer.

We need a simple calculation scheme to generate offers in a non-arbitrary manner, with the assurance that each subsequent offer, if higher than the previous one, is justifiably the best "compromise" among the prices.

The buyer needs to primarily make offers of prices ($p_1, p_2,$ and p_3) to the sellers, given fixed quantities of compensation components, namely, land area (M), number of sellers (N), and number of rehabilitation packages (Q). The offer would be made on the basis of the total budget, b, available to the buyer:

$$b = p_1 M + p_2 N + p_3 Q \tag{1}$$

We consider these quantities as being fixed because the acquisition is not equivalent to a speculative market commodity purchase, in which a buyer could have determined a "best" batch quantity based on market prices so as to achieve the desired level of utility U.

Instead, here we perceive that the quantities of land (area), the numbers of sellers and a minimum number of rehabilitation packages have been arrived at after due consideration of the common good, and that there is no other possibility for the buyer to purchase surplus land. Equally, there is the recognition that the transaction may not go through at all unless a minimum area of land is purchased. Hence, these quantities are fixed ahead of the process of generating a price offer in our case. Even more serious could be the task of estimating the utility U, since the buyer is not really concerned with such a quantity trade-off at all.

Also, prices are hardly "market" prices in our case of land acquisition. In fact, even a notional "land market" allowing for standardized pricing to be applied, in a case where the intent is to change the land use from agriculture to industry, does not exist in the country. Per unit area prices offered by the buyer need to be specifically customized for each type of acquisition environment, most often with very little prior history and knowledge of such prices in the same geographical area.

In this paper, we propose a somewhat fresh approach to building a buyer model. We propose that the buyer generate offers by minimizing a price trade-off function subject to a budget constraint in the general form:

$$\min v_b = f(p_1, p_2, p_3)$$
$$st$$
$$b = p_1 M + p_2 N + p_3 Q \tag{2}$$

where v is the price trade-off function that captures the concept that if the buyer is prepared to pay a higher price on one item, he will try to reduce the price offer on any or all of the others. The function v is intended to capture the trade-off between prices in a manner that enables the buyer to choose price offers that satisfy the budget equation while at the minimum v.

We now postulate that it would be possible to represent the buyer's interests while generating an offer on his behalf if we minimize the impact of trade-offs between the three rates by using the following function:

$$P_b = k_1 p_1^2 + k_2 p_2^2 + k_3 p_3^2 - k_4 p_1 p_2 - k_5 p_1 p_3 - k_6 p_2 p_3, \tag{3}$$

while meeting a budget constraint:

$$B_b = p_1 M + p_2 N + p_3 Q \tag{4}$$

In the price trade-off function in (3), the last three terms express the fact that, for a given value P_b, a price change in one direction should result in the other prices (in pairs) moving in the opposite direction The squared functions of the individual prices seek to ensure that the first three terms attempt to pull up the value of the overall price trade-off function when prices rise rapidly.

In order to visualize the impact of the trade-offs, we can view a 2D function of form (3), viz., $z(p_1, p_2) = p_1^2 + p_2^2 - p_1 p_2$ for values of p_1 and p_2 in the range of 0 through 10.

Figure 2. 2D Price function example

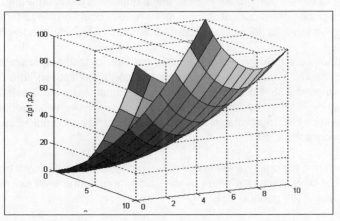

Note how the function curves up at larger values of p_1 and p_2. The prices chosen to minimize P_b need to satisfy the budget equation (4) where the quantities M, N and Q represent, respectively, the total size of the land in hectares, the number of sellers, and the number of rehabilitation packages to be offered.

It is fairly straightforward to determine such a price combination by constructing the Lagrangian:

$$V_b = (k_1 p_1^2 + k_2 p_2^2 + k_3 p_3^2 - k_4 p_1 p_2 - k_5 p_1 p_3 - k_6 p_2 p_3 + \lambda (p_1 M + p_2 N + p_3 Q - B_b) \quad (5)$$

and solving for the unknown prices and the Lagrangian multiplier λ from the set of linear equations resulting from:

$$\frac{\partial V_b}{\partial p_1} = 2k_1 p_1 \quad k_4 p_2 \quad k_5 p_3 + \lambda M = 0$$

$$\frac{\partial V_b}{\partial p_2} = 2k_2 p_2 \quad k_4 p_1 \quad k_6 p_3 + \lambda N = 0$$

$$\frac{\partial V_b}{\partial p_3} = 2k_3 p_3 \quad k_5 p_1 \quad k_6 p_2 + \lambda Q = 0$$

$$\frac{\partial V_b}{\partial \lambda} = p_1 M + p_2 N + p_3 Q \quad B_b = 0$$

$$(6)$$

In principle, the buyer need not know the explicit form of the trade-off between the prices but only express the relative importance of trade-offs by setting the values of $k_1 \ldots$ k_6 on the basis of an initial starting value for the ratios of the proposed prices. V_b, the price function itself is convex in certain price ranges and exhibits a minimum in the price space in that range, for suitably selected values of $k_1 \ldots k_5$.

Solving for (6) in the form:

$$
\begin{bmatrix}
2k_1 & k_4 & k_5 & M \\
k_4 & 2k_2 & k_6 & N \\
k_5 & k_6 & 2k_3 & Q \\
M & N & Q & 0
\end{bmatrix}
\begin{bmatrix}
p_1 \\
p_2 \\
p_3 \\
\lambda
\end{bmatrix}
=
\begin{bmatrix}
0 \\
0 \\
0 \\
B_b
\end{bmatrix}
\tag{7}
$$

yields a batch of prices p_i, $i=1\ldots3$ for a given budget B_b. That the price function exhibits a basic trade-off property between prices can be illustrated by setting the budget constant and generating new values of, say, p_2, and p_3, for increasing pre-set values for p_1 through an additional constraint in (7) as shown in the pseudo-code below. A plot of the values of p_1, p_2, and p_3 generated using the pseudo-code exhibits the trade-off property as shown in figure 3.

```
{
pr = 0.005;
for i=1:40{
```

$$
\begin{bmatrix}
2k_1 & k_4 & k_5 & M & 1 \\
k & 2k_2 & k_6 & N & 0 \\
k_5 & k_6 & 2k_3 & Q & 0 \\
M & N & Q & 0 & 0 \\
1 & 0 & 0 & 0 & 0
\end{bmatrix}
\begin{bmatrix}
p_1 \\
p_2 \\
p_3 \\
\lambda_1 \\
\lambda_2
\end{bmatrix}
=
\begin{bmatrix}
0 \\
0 \\
0 \\
B_b \\
pr
\end{bmatrix}
$$

```
pr*=1.05;
record p1,p2,p3, and v;

}
}
```

Figure 3. Price trade-off illustration

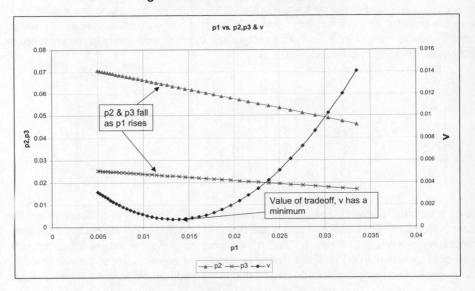

The plot of the values generated by the pseudo-code captures the non-linear trade-off in the convex price function, v, with the values of p_2 and p_3 falling as p_1 rises. The buyer model then essentially provides the basic mechanics to generate new price offers, given a budget, and quantity data. These prices are communicated to OE as the initial offer.

We shall shortly see how the buyer model accommodates changes to make a series of offers in response to the feedback from the sellers. But first, let us proceed with this initial cycle, and examine how the sellers might react to the offer.

Seller valuation models

From the seller's viewpoint, the primary concern is to ensure that the valuation for land compensates for both the land's perceived asset value and the potential losses in livelihood, wage income, and income from cultivation of the land parcel. For this purpose, we need to arrive at measures of income, wages and opportunity purely from a farmers' perspective.

The compensation should then address the following key concerns:

(a) The offer for the land should at least be better than the "market" value as perceived by the selling community;

(b) There should be a component that compensates for lost income from the cultivation and sales of produce from the land;

(c) There should be a component that compensates for equivalent family wages lost due to the sale of the land;

(d) There should be a component that provides for socio-economic development of the seller community as a whole.

On an individual seller basis, the important parts are items (a) to (c) above. We shall consider (d) later.

Let us start with the offer for the land itself. Let L_{min} denote a base price for land in the region, derivable possibly from the government's guidance value. Considering that the current offer from the buyer is p_1 (as communicated by OE), the seller j $(j = 1, \ldots N)$ seeks to maximize benefit from the difference:

$$w_j^1 = ls_j(p_1 - L_{min}) \tag{8}$$

where ls_j represents the land size owned by seller j. Obviously, if p_1 is lower even than the guidance value L_{min}, the offer will be rejected outright by the seller. That takes care of the first component of the compensation.

The second component concerns farm income. Surveys of regional farm production and yields available with several government agencies offer an initial guidance value, over which it is perfectly legitimate to allow for further enhancements based on local conditions. We assume that the OE can collect and collate local information for the calculation of basic projected income in the form:

$$w_j^2 = (rev_j - cost_j)(1 - r)^n \tag{9}$$

where w_j^2 denotes an estimate of profitability derived from estimates of revenue, rev_j and cost, $cost_j$, for seller j, should it be invested and grown over a period of n years at an interest rate of r per cent per annum. We postulate that each seller holds an expectation that this compensation will legitimately offset prospective gains that he would have made had he not sold the land.

We would also consider that loan liabilities not exceeding 25 per cent of the cost of the land per seller would be compensated as well.

In principle, a sum of the amounts of compensation in (8) and (9), together with the loan compensation above, should represent the overall expectation for each farmer. However, we should now consider the fact that the expectations can vary quite a bit depending on the actual values in (8) and (9), dependent as it is on the size of the land holding.

The size of a holding, for example, for a marginal farmer being of the order of about a hectare, the net compensation for land is expectedly small. For instance, a marginal farmer with 0.3 hectare may get in the neighbourhood of $4,800 in compensation for land even at $16,000 per hectare, and his wage compensation offer is likely to be in the range of $2,000 at best. For such a farmer, the attraction to land is clearly likely to be higher than for a large farmer, whose land compensation is surely likely to be several times the net wages for a family of his economic class.

In sum, the level of satisfaction with compensation components is likely to be less at smaller values of compensation, while more flexibility with offers is likely to be demonstrated when land holdings are large and consequent net compensations are large.

In order to capture this type of economic behaviour, we propose to calculate overall individual utility from compensation for seller j in the form:

$$u_j = q_1 \frac{(w_j^1)^{\gamma_1}}{\gamma_1} + q_2 \frac{(w_j^2)^{\gamma_2}}{\gamma_2} + l_j \tag{10}$$

where q_1 and q_2 are tuneable weights endowing differing degrees of importance to land compensation and other types of compensation, and l_j denotes the equivalent of a loan waiver subject to certain conditions. The impact of raising the compensation sums w_j^1 and w_j^2 to the power of γ_1 and γ_2 respectively, and dividing by the latter constants offers an interesting "saturation" effect when the constants are less than 1.

Shown in figure 4 is a plot of the function $f(w) = \dfrac{w^{\gamma}}{\gamma}$ against w on one axis for three different values of γ ($\gamma_1 = 0.3$, $\gamma_2 = 0.5$ and $\gamma_3 = 0.7$). Note that, for small values of w, the curves rise rapidly and flatten out at larger values of w. Plotted on the second axis is a set of graphs for the slopes over the same range of w, computed easily as:

$$f'(w) = \frac{d(f(w))}{dw} = w^{\gamma-1} \tag{11}$$

The slopes also show how a degree of saturation sets in at higher values of w, allowing us to accommodate the notion that small farmers with smaller values of w may "want more", while small changes in the total value may not impact the perceived value of the deal in the case of large farmers.

Another benefit from this class of utility function in our case is that we now have the facility of using different values of γ to differentiate between farmers with different land holdings to express their degree of satisfaction with the achievement of the desired utility. The lower the γ, the sooner (in the sense that even for smaller values of w), the achievement of satisfaction.

We thus utilize this function to construct the overall seller utility in the following form in (10).

Figure 4. Plot of f(w) and f '(w) for different γ

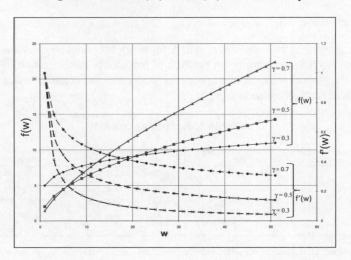

Using individual seller data it is possible to construct the value of u_j for every prospective seller. Note that two price levels p_1 and p_2 in the original seller offer are utilized to calculate the u_j's.

What remains now is to specify a mechanism for rating deviations of the calculated u_j's from a reference that each seller needs to have for himself. The degree of under- or overachievement should provide us with a rating scale that expresses the seller's level of agreement with the compensation packages and his affirmation to sell his parcel.

We propose that each seller employ two simple references. The first is the level of overachievement of the offer for land alone over u_j, expressed as a percentage over the land compensation, i.e.:

$$c_j^1 = (lcomp_j \quad u_j)/lcomp_j) \text{ where } lcomp_j = ls_j p_1, \ ls_j \text{ being the land size of seller } j.$$

Another reference is required to rate the wage compensation component. Suppose the net family wage income is estimated as wg_j, comprising annual wages for all working members of the family, whether from labour in their own land or other land which is under the acquisition plan, we expect the wage compensation to be calculated on a per seller basis as before:

$$fam\_wg_j = \frac{(wg_j(1+r)^n)^{\gamma_4}}{\gamma_4} \tag{12}$$

in a manner that accounts for invested future worth of the wages, subject to a treatment similar to previous utility calculations. This value can then be compared with the actual offer made by the buyer, which is simply p_2.

Each seller will then need to obtain his own measure of achievement

$$c_j^2 = (fam\_wg_j \quad p_2)/p_2 \tag{13}$$

We propose that the values of c^1 and c^2 for every seller not be disclosed to the buyer in a direct way so that the bargaining position of the sellers is not compromised. Instead, the numbers may be converted into a lexicographically ordered scale for use as a rule base. An example is illustrated below in table 1.

Table 1. Response gradati

c^1	Response-L	c^2	Response-W
$0<c^1<=0.1$	Very poor	$0<c^2<=0.1$	Very poor
$0.1<c^1<=0.2$	Poor	$0.1<c^2<=0.2$	Poor
$0.2<c^1<=0.3$	Satisfactory	$0.2<c^2<=0.3$	Satisfactory
$0.3<c^1<=0.4$	Good	$0.3<c^2<=0.4$	Good
$c^1>0.4$	Very Good	$c^2>0.4$	Very Good

Note: Response "L" is associated with land compensation, and Response "W" is associated with wage compensation.

By conveying responses in such scales calculated from the rule engine without actually revealing how they are arrived at, it becomes the responsibility of the buyer to work out by how much the offer may need to be improved before a seller will agree to the transaction.

Before we can set up full negotiation cycles, we need to determine how the buyer model can evaluate the scale-equivalent of c^1 and c^2, i.e the responses L (associated with land compensation) and W (associated with wage compensation) respectively, as defined in table 1, to make the next offer. For this we will need to go back briefly into the buyer model.

Buyer model revisited

It is in the interest of the buyer to tactically offer higher levels for wage and other types of compensation first, keeping the land price just at par with market prices. One should expect that the buyer will start the negotiations with some informal minimal proportions for the three components in mind. As an example, he could start by setting apart $a_1 = (p_2 * N + p_3 *Q) = 20$ per cent of the budget B_b, suggesting that the land compensation component would be 80 per cent of the total outlay. The buyer might set up an initial budget, choose an initial a_1, and make the rate offers to OE.

The OE assists in working out the L and W responses of all N farmers, and communicates the consolidated responses back to the buyer. The buyer needs to do some basic grouping of responses to determine, for example:

• The percentage of N that fell into each class of c^1 and c^2

- The percentage of N that might accept the wage compensation and land offer

- The percentage of N that might accept the wage and NOT the land offer, and vice versa

This analysis should help the buyer decide how to modify the offer and by how much. The buyer can next be expected to want to see if the number of sellers who accepted, say, the wage compensation increases merely by increasing a_1 (increasing the initial proportion) without actually increasing the overall budget. Note that the buyer is not informed of the individual responses of the sellers; the buyer only receives a group report that indicates how many sellers in any category responded to what level.

The buyer recognizes that, once an offer is made, reducing it for any component will be difficult unless some other component is made substantially more attractive. Hence, the buyer can be expected to increase the offer only in small increments.

The buyer is usually constrained by the fact that, unless a very large proportion of the land—say 90 per cent—is covered by the sellers giving a high ranking to values L and W, the transaction may not close. Hence, he will attempt to get concurrence on a component that costs him less before proceeding to budget more on other components. For instance, suppose that he discovers that all the sellers will agree to his current wage compensation offer, $w = p_2{}^*N$; he will introduce this equation as a new constraint into his original model. This will only add an additional λ parameter into the set of equation (6). The solution effectively "continues" setting wage compensation to the agreed level.

It is critical to note that the buyer is not allowed to make separate offers to "obdurate" sellers, whether in terms of wage compensation or for land. Equity demands that the rate of land be the same, while wage compensation may be customizable to individual seller's socio-graphics—but even that must be done in a transparent manner.

One final point, before we examine real negotiation cycles and data, is about the third component of compensation—the Rehabilitation Package. This package is for the entire seller community and cannot be appropriated by individual sellers. Hence, its utility needs to be assessed by the seller community in coordination with an agency that has the expertise to analyse and explain the offer to the community. This is typically a task for an NGO.

Once there is overall agreement between the buyer and the seller on rates, there is a need for a financial intermediary to step in and coordinate transactions between them in concert with the OE and the NGO. We envisage that the services of this intermediary would not be for profit and would probably be ideally suited to an established bank in the public sector. Given that the transactions can take place over a period of time and may include annuity type of payments in part, there is a need for an entity to play the role of guarantor to avoid situations where the buyer and some sellers may backtrack after the agreement is reached.

Broadly, therefore, the economic utility models that we have explored for the buyer and the seller need to play out the negotiation cycle within a process framework, which includes the additional entities mentioned above. The original schema of figure 1 can thus be enhanced to include these entities, as shown in figure 5 below.

Figure 5. Enhanced structure of entities for negotiation

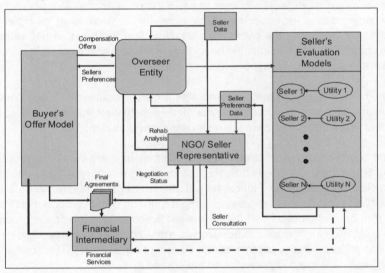

We envisage that the role of a seller's representative who can speak with the OE on behalf of the sellers and vice-versa is a critical one, for that representative will have the necessary information from other entities to explore and discuss seller-level issues and explain the impact of choices to individual sellers. This entity will also have the data to analyse the rehabilitation package for the socio-economic development of the community as a whole.

The financial intermediary is expected to play a larger role only after the final agreement is reached between other parties. As mentioned, it needs to play the role of guarantor and facilitator, and offer the services of a banker to the sellers. We shall revisit these issues following explorations into simulated negotiations in the next section.

III. DATA FOR SIMULATION OF NEGOTIATIONS

This section describes data sets we created for simulation experiments with the above buyer and seller models. As can be expected, the composition of sizes of land parcels, and the pattern of ownership will play a significant role in the negotiations. Hence, we shall consider two different scenarios: one with a rather high degree of fragmentation of land, somewhat mirroring the situation in, for example, Singur in West Bengal (Sau 2008), and a second where the land parcels are somewhat larger.

In order to obtain a realistic situation, we have generated data on a number of demographic and sociographic variables, the principal among which are given in table 2.

Table 2. Baseline seller data

Variable	Type	Remarks
Seller_ID	number	Identifier
Lsize	number	Land size in hectare
Ltype	alphanumeric	Land Type Classifier: a1: Multi-crop, irrigated; a2: Single Crop, irrigated, etc [Used to calculate potential yield]
Ctype	alpha	Crop-season identifier
Cost	number	Estimated input cost in United States dollars per hectare [Depends on combination of ctype and ltype; does not include wages for family labour]
Rev	number	Estimated revenue from sale of output in dollars per hectare [Depends on ctype, and estimated market prices]
Fsize	number	Number of members in seller's family [Counted once only, even if more than one plot is owned by the family]
wgincome	number	Estimated income from wages when family members work in their own or other land holdings under consideration for acquisition
regcost	number	Declared land value under registration system in United States dollars
Louts	number	Outstanding current loan burden on family as a whole

Source: Variable definitions used for model development by the authors

Cost and revenue numbers need to be estimated on the basis of a combination of crop-type and land-type. In our experiment, we assume that the contiguous land the buyer seeks is about 800-1,000 hectares in a single geographic area, allowing the possibility of nearly identical soil, weather and fertility conditions, with differences in cost and revenue arising merely from subtle variations in cropping patterns.

In order to mirror a realistic situation, we have considered the following pattern data for small, marginal and large farmers shown in table 3.

Table 3. Illustrative crop pattern data

Type of Farmer	Land Holding	Crop Pattern
Marginal	<= 1 hectare	high yielding rice kharif crop followed by rabi rice
Small	>1<=2 hectare	high yielding rice kharif crop followed by mustard
Medium/Large	> 4 hectare	high yielding rice kharif crop followed by potato

Source: Farmer and cropping pattern classification used for model development by the authors

The yield and price data for such a scenario has been referenced and based on published sources (Maji and others 1995). Using this baseline data, we created two cases differing in the distribution of land holding. Case 1 offers a scenario with a higher degree of fragmentation than case 2.

Case 1

The distribution of land in this case is shown in table 4.

Table 4. Land distribution for case 1

Number of sellers	Land holding (hectare)	Remarks
500	.2 - .4	Marginal
100	.41 - .6	Marginal
40	.61 - .85	Marginal
10	.86 – 1.0	Marginal
160	1.1 - 1.4	Small
90	1.41 - 1.6	Small
40	1.61 - 1.85	Small
10	1.86 - 1.99	Small
40	2.1 - 5	Medium/Large
6	5.1- 6	Medium/Large
4	>6	Medium/Large

Figure 6. Cumulative land distribution pattern

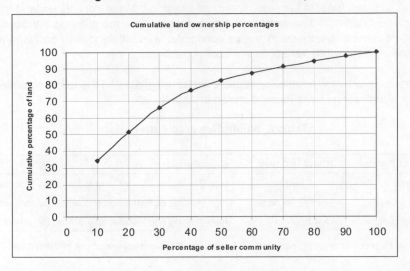

The distribution is plotted in the form of cumulative proportion above. With about 83 per cent of the land owned by 50 per cent of the community, and about 65 per cent of 1,000-strong seller community being marginal farmers, this clearly represents a case where the degree of fragmentation is rather high.

Case 2

The distribution of land in this case is shown in table 5.

Table 5. Land distribution for case 2

No. of sellers	Total land size (in hectare)	Remarks
115	100	Marginal farmers
118	200	Small farmers
79	700	Medium/large farmers

The farmers in case 2 are better placed economically with just one fourth of them holding about 70 per cent of the land. As the land is not very fragmented, it is expected that the buyer will spend less to acquire these 1,000 hectares.

IV. THE NEGOTIATION PROCESS MODEL

In this section, we shall put together all the elements of the buyer and seller models discussed above into a more formal description of the process.

We believe that the negotiation process should ideally comprise four phases: (a) preparatory or pre-negotiation; (b) negotiation; (c) execution; and (d) evaluation. It is quite possible that acquisition tasks in many practical cases, and even in those cases that have resulted in failure, have indeed broadly followed these descriptions. However, we would like to place emphasis on formally outlining the tasks in these phases, particularly the conditions that must be examined at the beginning and end of each phase. The conditions are meant to provide a set of simple tests that tell us if the process is moving satisfactorily and if there might be issues that can stymie the land acquisition exercise.

Preparatory pre-negotiation phase

In this phase, all parties concerned with the acquisition are identified, and data pertaining to the land, seller community, buyer, Overseer, local authorities, NGO etc. is shared and verified. Key participants need to formally agree on:

1. Extents and ownership of land proposed to be acquired;
   a. Componentization of Compensation into
      i. Land Compensation
         • Minimum Price for Land

ii. Wage and Other Per-Seller Compensation
  ● Minimum Rate for Wage Compensation
ii. Rehabilitation Package for Whole Seller Community
  ● Minimum number of packages and rates

2. Principle that the negotiation shall follow prescribed procedures
  a. with specified disclosures of information;
  b. with prescribed ownership of information;
  c. with prescribed exit conditions
    i. for Buyer
    ii. for Seller Community

We shall not delve into the details of the preparatory phase, as that would require describing legal and other steps that would be outside the scope of this paper. It is sufficient to state that the tests to determine whether agreement has been achieved between parties on authenticity, integrity and completeness of data have yielded positive results, and parties agreed to proceed with negotiations on the basis of acknowledged minimum values of component compensation rates.

Negotiation processes

The negotiation process involving the buyer and the seller through the overseer entity is pictured in the flow diagram shown in figure 7.

Figure 7. Negotiation process and communications

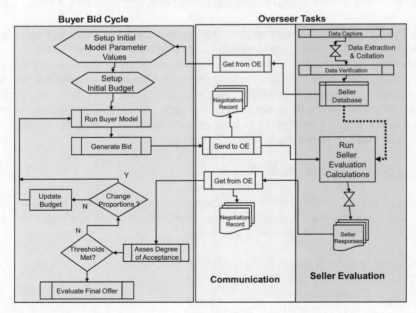

The OE clearly needs to perform both the tasks of initial data capture and collation from the sellers so that it has all data to play the intermediary role in negotiations. The buyer model is set up using inputs from this database. An initial budget (typically arrived at on the basis of agreed minimum rates) is set up by the buyer to run the model and generate the first bid, which is then sent to the OE.

The OE uses this bid to work out compensations on a per seller basis, which is conveyed to individual sellers together with calculated levels of achievement of the utilities. The responses c^1 and c^2 are converted to levels L and W using a pre-agreed range scale. At this time, the OE in consultation with individual seller may allow specific tuning of L and W within pre-agreed limits.

The responses are sent back to the buyer, who then assesses the degree of acceptance, applying his own criteria to judge whether to tweak the proportions of compensation, keeping the same overall budget, or to increase budget.

This done, the next cycle bid calculation and communication is started. It is up to the buyer to decide when to stop making further offers, expectedly based on an internal and undisclosed constraint on the overall budget. For instance, if the buyer finds that, say 95 per cent the owners of say, 95 per cent of the land parcels have agreed to sell at the current bid, and acquisition of the remaining 5 per cent may come only at a significantly higher price, the buyer may choose to stop the negotiations and try to close the deal at this stage. It is obviously up to the sellers to determine how much they might be able to stretch the buyer's bid.

The exit conditions can also be pre-agreed, in that the buyer and the sellers can agree on an outer limit for rates as well, even before negotiations start. Exit clauses can also include conditions that put an upper limit on the number of cycles or the threshold percentage of land up to which wage compensation will not be increased, and many more such variations.

V. RESULTS

We shall present the results of negotiation cycles with data in case 1. As will be recalled, this case has a higher degree of fragmentation.

Case 1

The total land parcel owned by 1,000 sellers in this case is 860.41 hectares. Table 6 shows the values of $\gamma_1,...\gamma_4$ that we have set in the individual utility functions for the sellers in this experiment.

Table 6. Settings for gammas

Seller type	γ_1	γ_2	γ_3	γ_4
Marginal farmer	0.8	0.6	0.6	0.8
Small farmer	0.7	0.7	0.7	0.7
Large farmer	0.6	0.8	0.8	0.5

The values of γ for marginal farmers and small farmers have been set higher than those of large farmers to reflect the perceived notional attraction to land, since farmers with only a small holding expect small total compensations, which can nevertheless be several times their annual income, their attraction to the land parcel can be considered to be stronger. Hence, γ saturation will occur far more slowly, i.e. their behaviour is better represented by higher values of γ. On the other hand, sellers with larger land holdings may be expected to be less sensitive to small changes in the price since the total compensation expected is itself large, while their annual income from the land itself is also large. Hence, we have set smaller γ values for them in our experiments.

We initiate the buyer offer process with a starting budget value of $12 million. The manner in which the price offer increases in response to the seller valuations is shown in figure 8.

Figure 8. Evolution of bid prices during negotiations (case 1)

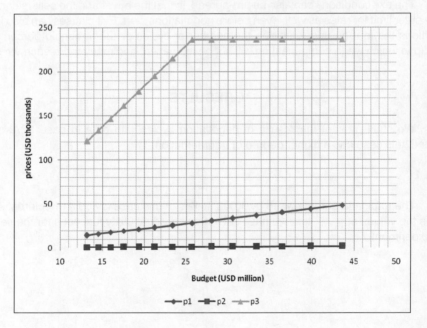

The buyer has increased the price p_3 for the rehab package (the green curve) from about \$120,000 to about \$237,000 over eight cycles, until receiving acceptance from all sellers. During these cycles, the buyer model has maintained p_2, the price for wage compensation constant, and increased land prices marginally to accommodate the large percentage of sellers who have demanded more on this account. Beyond the eighth cycle, the buyer has held both these prices at the last offer price and increased land prices over the next eight cycles until acceptance by all sellers at the final price of p_1=\$48,000/ha, p_2=\$1,833 (approx.) of wage compensation per seller, and p_3=\$237,000 for payment towards the rehabilitation package. The total payout proposed by the buyer model is \$43.56 million, of which land compensation alone is about 95.2 per cent, the bill for wage compensation for all 1,000 sellers is 4.2 per cent, and the rehabilitation package for the community of sellers is 0.54 per cent.

The sellers have evaluated the offer against their utilities as conveyed acceptance using c^1 and c^2 over the 16 cycles in the trajectory graphed below.

Figure 9. Growth of acceptance proportions during negotiations (case 1)

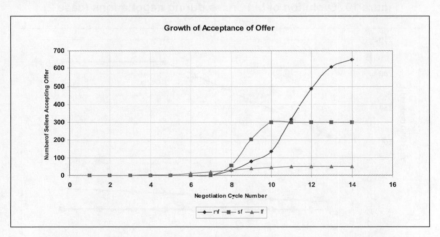

It is interesting to note that the large farmers (green curve) have begun to convey overall acceptance starting from cycle 6, and nearly all have accepted the offers by the eleventh cycle. The small farmers (pink curve) begin to find the offer satisfactory only a cycle later, and all accept the offer just a cycle ahead of the large farmers. But it is clearly the marginal farmers (blue curve) with very small land holdings who appear to hold out until the last cycle, with only about 50 per cent of them accepting the current offers at the eleventh cycle.

As can be seen at this late stage of the negotiation (eleventh cycle), it has been the land price that has been the stumbling block for the vast majority of the marginal farmers, while the other farmers owning large land parcels have clearly begun to accept the current offers.

Hence, our model, offer evaluation, and response evaluation process appear to have captured the notion that sellers with very small land holdings often have a stronger attraction to land because it may be their only livelihood, while owners of larger holdings become less sensitive to small changes in land prices because their overall land compensation sizes become larger, and the wage or other compensations become less significant at this stage.

It is again no surprise that the simulation experiment points to more protracted negotiations due to a large number of marginal farmers in the community of sellers—i.e., the land parcel is more fragmented.

We shall now examine the situation prevailing when the land is less fragmented.

Case 2

In this data set, we have fewer marginal farmers. The price growth chart for the negotiation cycles is simulated in figure 10.

Figure 10. Evolution of bid prices during negotiations (case 2)

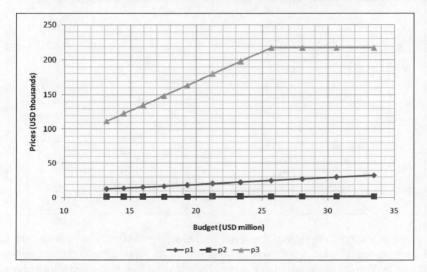

The negotiation cycles, starting with a budget of $12 million, are completed in just 11 cycles in case 2, with a final settlement value of $33.44 million (over $10 million less than in case 1). Full acceptance for wage compensation and rehabilitation appears to come by as early as the eighth and fifth cycles respectively.

The total land bill for the buyer in this deal is 97.38 per cent of the above total compensation package, while the other two packages are 1.95 per cent and 0.65 per cent respectively. The final agreed price for land works out to about $32,570/ha. The lower land price is a consequence of the softer bargain driven by the bulk of a larger number of large land owners, as can be seen in figure 11.

Figure 11. Growth of acceptance proportions during negotiations (case 2)

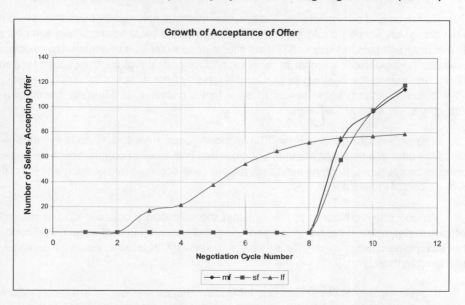

The acceptance behaviour of the small and marginal farmers is somewhat similar in this case, with the bulk of them accepting the offer over the last three cycles. The large farmers, forming about 25 per cent of the seller community in case 2, begin to accept the offers in small groups starting from the second cycle until all of them agree gradually over the next eight to nine cycles.

The fact that there was significantly less fragmentation of land in case 2 has clearly helped in getting the buyer a larger land parcel (1,000 hectares distributed over 312 sellers) at a lower price per hectare, as well as lower total compensation.

The problem with higher fragmentation is that there are a larger number of individual utilities to achieve, which constitute a larger compensation sum even though they are individually smaller.

VI. CONCLUDING REMARKS: POLICY RECOMMENDATIONS

The central objective of this work has been to explore the possibility of building a mathematical foundation for negotiations between a buyer and a community of sellers for acquisition of agricultural land. In the Indian context, this class of transactions has been surrounded by a variety of controversies, primarily emanating from the lack of an established, regulated, transparent and fair mechanism for negotiations between buyers and sellers. The valuations of land and processes for making and communicating offers have generally been *ad hoc*.

To the best of our knowledge, the practical methods followed by buyers today do not go beyond a very simplified rule: (a) find minimum guidance value from different sources; (b) add minimum solatium; (c) make offer. If the offer is unacceptable, as evidenced by reluctance to sell, the buyer decides whether to raise the offer or back out of the transaction for good. It is not uncommon for a variety of problems—ranging from a "hold out" among sellers, to partial collusion among some sellers to seek better prices, to a complete breakdown of transactions—to arise at this stage.

The sellers of agricultural land have mostly been rural folk without the means to assess the offer in a scientific manner. The pulls and pressures of community dynamics and individual compulsions, such as outstanding loans, and declining family incomes often drive the decisions of individuals.

Among other criticisms is the fact that the valuation processes do not prescribe methods to determine if the compensation adequately covered loss of wages, livelihood, or other income-generating means for the sellers, particularly those who would be parting with small landholdings.

Considerations of compensations for lost livelihoods and wages are rarely reflected in the final figures unless political or other pressures are brought into the picture. It is indeed rare for the compensation to cover community development activities, such as common infrastructure facilities for roads, health care, hygiene, education or vocational training.

In this paper, we have taken the approach that the solution needs to be arrived by considering actions from three different angles, with a legal framework that stipulates basic rules of engagement:

1. That, in cases where land parcels to be acquired are larger than a few hundred hectares of agricultural land fragmented beyond a specified limit, compensation must have at least three components, viz, land, wages, community development; the latter two components may be considered for payment in annuity form;

2. That it must become statutory to have certain identified entities that provide regulatory, overseer, ombudsman, financial and communication services between buyers and sellers;

3. That a process workflow be followed, which takes information generated in the negotiation in a systematic manner between the parties involved, maintaining transparency where it is required and security of information where it is required;

4. That a set of agreed mathematical models be deployed for:

   a. The buyer to generate the offers;

   b. The sellers to evaluate the offers;

   c. The conversion of seller valuations to scaled ranges of variables which the buyer can interpret to generate the subsequent offers.

The focus of this paper was primarily on the last two of the above. We stated the critical requirements for (1) underscoring the need for setting up the entities for achieving the requirements in (2). We then proposed models that might satisfy the requirement for (3). Among the key issues in setting up the models, we have attempted to address the problem of a mechanism for generating offers by the buyer. The offers are evaluated using individual utilities of the sellers, and converted to usable responses by the seller, in order to accept a modified offer in another cycle of negotiation.

In this paper, we have proposed a price-trade-off driven model for the buyer, which allows the generation of price offers in a manner that is not *ad hoc* nor requires serious knowledge of downstream cost factors. For instance, a buyer might need to set up only upper and lower limits for prices on the basis of detailed information on future use of the land (after industry is set up, etc.). But generating a price offer for the land within these limits is only seen as a question of obtaining a good trade-off between price components, given the acceptance criteria of the sellers. The seller model thus uses only information local to the offer model and its components. The parameters in the model offer more than enough flexibility to enable it to be applied to different situations.

We also explore methods whereby the seller can evaluate the offer on an individual basis, using data pertaining to that individual within the seller community. Here, we have explored setting up utility functions, which can be fine tuned to the needs of individual sellers. Using the value of γ, for instance, to tune the degree of satisfaction helps capture the possible higher attraction for land among marginal farmers, for whom its loss might even take away their only source of livelihood.

While we have considered several variables, such as size of family and income from land, several others could easily be added to refine the valuation of a land parcel in practical circumstances—for instance, number of trees, number of water sources (such as borewells), shed/barns, and a soil fertility index. We have also considered the possibility of evaluating wage or other cash compensations in the form of a future value over a period of time. This may be of particular relevance to marginal landowners.

The translation of the acceptance criteria at individual seller levels to a five-point scale was done here to illustrate the process of communication between the buyer and the sellers. Obviously, many alternative mechanisms could be devised. However, the objective here was to ensure that the bargaining position of individual sellers, contained in the limiting values of their utilities, would not be revealed to the buyer, for then he would naturally try to just meet it. Without that knowledge, the buyer might even exceed it, benefiting the selling community as a whole. In other words, the sellers can convey they want "more", without saying "how much more", while it becomes the buyer's responsibility to offer what he thinks is the lowest amount that might satisfy the largest number of sellers in that negotiation cycle. The other critical benefit is that the possibility of a "speculative hold out" is considerably reduced in this process because the buyer cannot track individual responses and the seller does not know how his response is impacting subsequent offers—only aggregate behaviour drives the bids.

Finally, it is important to mention that the process of negotiation will gain substantial credibility in the Indian context, if aside from NGOs and government regulatory body participation, there is a healthy role for government-backed financial institutions which can serve as an intermediary offering services to both buyer and seller parties. Its presence adds a significant value to the financial security of prospective transactions.

The simulation experiments we conducted with two sets of data appear to bring out the interesting relationship between higher compensations and higher fragmentation of land ownership patterns. While the increase has traditionally been associated with the additional burden of managing a larger group of sellers, there is really a cost associated with increased compensations for marginal landowners who have a higher "attraction" to their land, as theorized from a land assembly economics perspective (Evans 2004).

In our experiments with data representing a higher degree of fragmentation, the fact that the sellers in the small and marginal farmer category "held out" longer than the large farmers in anticipation of higher compensations is a result of the threshold settings on their utility functions in the simulation. In a practical exercise, one would like to set up the model parameters in manner that would closely mimic the behaviour of the sellers, and both our approach and the methodology described here offer such facilities. While economic theory (Evans 2004) indeed suggests that such behaviour should be expected, studies in several areas in India have shown an interesting contra-behaviour (Sanhati 2008). Marginal and small farmers in regions where agricultural productivities have plummeted seem to prefer to opt out of agriculture at first opportunity, and sometimes have settled for less.

In conclusion, this paper is an exploration into structured models and processes for acquisition of agricultural land. While there is much to be done towards establishing fair and transparent legal systems and regulatory frameworks in the Indian context, there is also a strong need to build structured models for generating and evaluating offers. Further work is intended to address issues related to group behaviour among prospective sellers, and how such behaviour might influence acceptance criteria.

REFERENCES

Agnihotri, Vipin (2007). "New Land Acquisition Act to disallow states to acquire land on behalf of private sector", *The India Street*, July.

Alias, Anuar and Md Nasir Daud (2007). "Payment of adequate compensation for land acquisition in Malaysia", *Pacific Rim Property Research Journal*, vol. 12, No. 3.

Banerjee, Abhijit Vinayak, P. Bardhan and K. Basu (2007). "Beyond Nandigram: Industrialization in West Bengal", *Economic and Political Weekly*, 28 April, pp. 1487-1489.

Basu, Pranab Kanti (2007). "The political economy of land grab", *Economic and Political Weekly*, 7 April, pp. 1281-1287.

Bhaduri, Amit (2007). "Alternatives in industrialization", *Economic and Political Weekly*, 5 May.

Bhaskar, Utpal (2008). "RIL's SEZ in Haryana in Scup over land cost", accessed from http://www.livemint.com/2008/07/08235419/.

BS-Edit (2008). "The 70:30 land acquisition formula", Business Standard, 23 October.

Chandra, Nirmal Kumar (2008). "Tata Motors in Singur: A step towards industrialization or pauperization", *Economic and Political Weekly,* vol. 43, Issue 50 (December), pp. 36-51.

Das, Debarshi (2006). "Land acquisition bill and the panchayet: Things to expect and fear: A case study on Salboni", Sanhati.

Dan, Pranab K, Kousik Guhathakurta, Shatadru Gupta (2008). "Modeling for land acquisition for SEZ", e-Journal of Science and Technology.

Das, Sanchita (2007). "Land acquisition issues stall industrial parks in West Bengal", accessed from http://www.livemint.com/ 2007/ 12/ 05230129.

Datta, Promita (2008). "Big-ticket projects struggle to acquire land in West Bengal", accessed from http://www.livemint.com/2008/06/ 16003000.

Debroy, Bibek (2008). "The land problem and Sin of Singur", IMI Interface, July-Sept.

Evans, A. (2004). *Economics, Real Estate and the Supply of Land*, (Oxford, Blackwell Publishing) p. 193.

Gupta, Sayantan (2008). "An overview of Land Acquisition at Singur", IndLaw.com.

India (2007a). "The Resettlement and Rehabilitation Bill", Draft of Bill 98, 2007.

India (2007b). "Land Acquisition (Amendment) Bill: Bill 97 of 2007.

Iyer, Ramaswamy (2007). "Towards a Just Displacement and Rehabilitation Policy", *Economic and Political Weekly*, 28 July, pp. 3103-3017.

Joshi, Sharad (2007). "Let farmers decide", *Hindu Business Line*, 26 December.

Maji, C.C., T. Haque and A. Bhattacharya (1995). "Small farms, employment and surplus generation - A case of West Bengal", NCAP Policy Paper No. 5, published by Director, NCAP.

Morris, Sebastian and A. Pandey (2007). "Towards reform of land acquisition framework in India, Working Paper No. 2007-05-04, IIM Ahmedabad, India.

Sangvai, Sanjay (2006). "Land-grab by the rich: The politics of SEZs in India", *The South Asian*, 5 July.

Sanhati Editorial (2008). "Do rural poor support land acquisition? A Survey by the Indian Statistical Institution".

Sau, Ranjit (2008). "A ballad of Singur: Progress with human dignity", Economic and Political Weekly, vol. 43, Issue 43 (October) pp. 10-11.

Srinivasan, Suresh (2008). "Industrial projects: Easing land acquisition pains", *Hindu Business Line*, 17 October.

Vijapurkar, Mahesh (2007a). "An innovative price mechanism for farmland acquisition", The Information Co Pvt Ltd., 6 April.

Vijapurkar, Mahesh (2007b). "Not low prices, but equity please", The Information Co Pvt Ltd., 22 March.

THE INFLUENCE OF TAX REFORMS ON THE PROSPERITY OF MICRO-FIRMS AND SMALL BUSINESSES IN UZBEKISTAN

Dildora Tadjibaeva and Iroda Komilova*

The article gives inside into tax system of Uzbekistan, a former Soviet republic. It analyses major tax reforms in the country since the early days of its independence (1991) with special attention given to the simplified method of taxation, used for micro-firms and small businesses (MSEs). The results of 30 in-depths interviews with representatives of MSEs revealed substantial reductions in tax rates (the average tax burden is 14.9 per cent) and overall improvements in the business environment. However, despite the numerous changes in Uzbek taxation, the issues related to tax administration (tax audits, reporting and competence of tax inspectors) make it difficult to operate in Uzbekistan without breaking rules. To be effective and successful, tax reform needs to be accompanied by institutional and structural reform throughout the economy.

I. INTRODUCTION

Since independence in 1991, Uzbekistan has pursued a gradual approach to the transition from a planned to a market economy. The Government aimed at building a socially oriented market economy and developing industrial and manufacturing capacity in a predominantly agricultural economy using substantial and direct central control (Gemayel and Grigorian 2005).

The tax system of Uzbekistan developed in line with the country's course of reforms, and the elements of a modern tax system, administrative and institutional capacity evolved in successive steps. This less-than-ideal tax reform was the result of a compromised to preserve government revenues in the early years of independence (Martinez-Vazques and McNab 2003).

Early tax reforms were mainly directed towards the fiscal role of taxation and underestimated its regulatory, social and stimulating roles. This short-term fiscal policy negatively affected private sector development, investment and employment and led to the rapid growth of an informal economy.

More recent reforms in taxation were directed towards reducing the tax burden, optimizing the structure and rates of taxes, simplifying and unifying the tax system, as well as increasing the stimulatory and regulatory functions of tax policy.

* Dr. Dildora Tadjibaeva is Deputy Director at the Center for Economic Development, Uzbekistan, and Iroda Komilova is a Senior Lecturer at Westminster International University in Tashkent, Uzbekistan.

From 2000 to 2007, the tax burden in the economy fell from 40 per cent to 27 per cent (Tuchkova 2008). This was achieved through consecutive reductions of federal and local tax rates, mandatory payments and the streamlining of taxes.

The small business sector plays an increasingly important role in Uzbekistan. According to the State Committee on Statistics, in 2008, small business accounted for 48.2 per cent of GDP and 76 per cent of total employment (Uzbekistan, 2008). Changes in tax legislation create favourable preconditions for the further development of small business. In 2007 alone, tax exemptions increased the financial resources of the business sector by 830 billion sums (Karimov 2008).

However, numerous amendments in Uzbek taxation do not yet testify to the creation of a perfect tax system, and this remains as one of the most complex aspects of Uzbekistan's business environment.

This study is divided into five sections. Section I analyses the development of the tax system in Uzbekistan since its independence in 1991, with special attention to the simplified method of taxation used for micro-firms and small businesses (MSEs). Section II develops research methodology and builds up primary data collection instrument for the study. Section III presents the findings of 30 in-depth interviews which were conducted with representatives of MSEs in five regions of Uzbekistan to explore the impact of recent tax reforms on business activities. Sections IV and V, the final part of the research, contain a list of conclusions and recommendations which are directed towards improving the business climate in Uzbekistan.

II. DEVELOPMENT OF THE TAX SYSTEM IN UZBEKISTAN

Over the past 18 years, the Uzbek tax system has gone through roughly four development phases:

Phase 1 – from 1991 to 1994;
Phase 2 – from 1995 to 1999;
Phase 3 – from 2000 to 2004;
Phase 4 – 2005 to the present.

Phase 1 (1991-1994)

In the early 1990s, Uzbekistan's economic situation was very fragile; consequently, the tax system was geared first of all to meet its *fiscal* targets. These targets were to be met against the backdrop of a rupture of economic relations, high inflation rates, a slump in production and a narrow taxable base. The deciding factor in the economic policy of 1991-1994 was the need to prevent a collapse of the economy, the sudden impoverishment of population and the stratification of society.

The share of GDP derived from private sector activities was very small in all transition countries early after independence. In Uzbekistan, it was less than 1 per cent (International Monetary Fund 1991)!

The process of transition from a centrally planned economy to a market one (Tanzi and Tsibouris 2000):

- Destroyed the plan and thus eliminated the information that the plan had provided on quantities produced and on prices at which the output was sold. The Government now had to rely on other sources, including the declarations of the taxpayers, to obtain this information. As a consequence, the prospect of tax evasion rose;

- Increased dramatically the number of producers and thus the number of potential taxpayers, as many private sector activities came into existence. Tax administrations that had been used to dealing with relatively few, friendly enterprises had to deal with hundreds of thousands or even millions of unfriendly taxpayers; [1]

- Much of the growth originated from the new small and difficult-to-tax private producers, who required scrutiny on the part of the tax authorities because of their high propensity for tax evasion. At the same time, these small producers required protection from unscrupulous tax officials (Kornai 1997).

These changes required the creation of a new tax system, laws, fiscal institutions and new skills. Fiscal institutions needed clear strategies and objectives, well-defined legal powers and well-defined legal obligations towards those taxpayers. An acute need was to develop the basic economic knowledge of government employees responsible for forming the new tax policy. Interestingly, during this stage, taxation was considered part of the responsibility of accountants and, consequently, at institutions of higher education, taxation was a component of accounting subjects.

These economic conditions in the country necessitated the implementation of new taxes and payments suitable for the transition period but the tax regime at this stage was not characterized by diversity of taxes (figure 1).

---

[1] In Soviet times, most individuals never had direct contact with the tax authorities. The majority of taxes were hidden from the people who ultimately bore them, with the result that most individuals were not even aware that, indirectly, they were paying a large amount of taxes. Thus, a "tax consciousness" or tax culture never developed.

Figure 1. Composition of taxes in government revenues, 1994

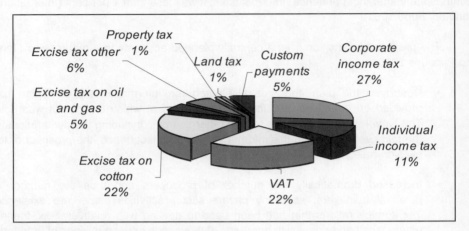

Source: Uzbekistan, Ministry of Finance, 1994.

Note: Extrabudgetary revenues were not included in government revenues.

During the first phase of reforms (and even in the later ones), some principles and practices of a socialistic tax system were observed in the Uzbek tax system (Martinez-Vazquez and McNab 2003):

- *Customized taxes:* Large tax payers could easily negotiate tax exemptions; [2]

- *Lack of a tradition of voluntary compliance:* Two fundamental pillars of modern tax systems, voluntary compliance and self-filing, were absent for Uzbek taxpayers (Kornai 1997);

- *Underdeveloped tax administration;*

- *Public distrust of government institutions:* The failure of government to raise general living standards combined with increased corruption among government officials encouraged taxpayers to move to a shadow economy. A high level of tax evasion affected compliant taxpayers and their perception of the fairness of the fiscal system, creating a vicious circle of *corruption, a high tax burden, and tax evasion.*

The need to maintain the relative stability of production and the reduction of inflation rates gave a start to the second round of reforms.

---

[2] A local car manufacturer, JV General Motors Uzbekistan, exports its cars at a zero rate of value-added tax (VAT), with no excise tax or duties paid.

Phase 2 (1995-1999)

The main achievement of the second stage was the development and adoption of the Tax Code in 1998. The Tax Code attempted to streamline taxes, reduce the burden on taxpayers, and simplify accounting and payment procedures. The establishment of the State Tax Committee at the beginning of 1998 was aimed at ensuring compliance from all taxpayers.

The tax policy of this period sought to maintain revenue collection while easing the tax burden on enterprises. In line with the latter objective, the Government reduced the profit tax rate from 36 per cent to 35 per cent in 1998 and to 33 per cent in 1999. In 1998, authorities eliminated the cotton excise tax in response to a decline in world cotton prices. To compensate for the impact of these changes on tax revenues, excise tax rates (in particular on energy products) and VAT rate were increased in 1998 and 1999.[3]

At the dawn of its activities, the State Tax Committee improved tax collection, which reduced arrears on profit taxes and significantly increased income tax revenue from the self-employed.[4]

Figure 2. Composition of taxes in government revenues, 1999

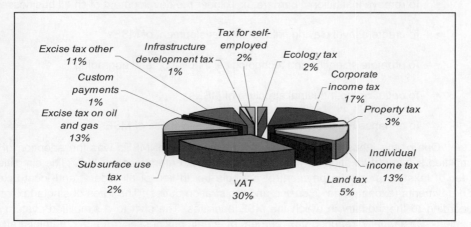

Source: Uzbekistan, Ministry of Finance, 1999.

Note: Extrabudgetary revenues were not included in government revenues.

---

[3] The standard VAT rate was increased from 18 per cent in 1997 to 20 per cent in 1998, and, in 1999, the preferential rate for food products was increased from 10 per cent to 15 per cent.

[4] The State Tax Committee has carried out strong disciplinary actions against corrupt officials and has improved collections from the informal sector (e.g., it streamlined the collection of fees from traders in bazaars).

Since 1997, Uzbekistan has followed a strategy of import substitution that has relied heavily on administrative intervention and a restrictive foreign exchange and trade regime in order to protect domestic producers from external competition (International Monetary Fund 2000).

As a result of the abovementioned policies, the business sector expanded significantly. By the end of the 1990s, small businesses comprised more than 80 per cent of all registered enterprises in Uzbekistan.

In 1999, MSEs contributed 23.8 per cent of GDP (Uzbekistan 2008a).

Realizing the significant role of small businesses in promoting fast and healthy economic and social development, the Government of Uzbekistan in 1999 started the structural transformation of the economy through the accelerated development of the private sector, especially small enterprises, and viewed it as a priority of government reforms.[5] The main mission of the Government during this period was to implement the small business promotion law, which involved the following tasks:[6]

- To further improve policies and measures concerning the development of MSEs;

- To remove institutional barriers that hinder the development of small businesses;

- To create a level playing field for the development of MSEs;

- To promote scientific and technological innovation and upgrading;

- To optimize the industrial structure of MSEs;

- To enhance the overall quality and competitiveness of MSEs.

One of the steps that promoted the development of MSEs was the adoption of a simplified system of taxation for micro-firms and small enterprises in 1998.[7] The simplified order of taxation proposed payment of a single tax in lieu of all federal and local taxes and payments (except trade, licensing and registration duties). The rates of single tax vary according to the industry in which the MSE operates. The shift to a simplified system of taxation substantially reduced tax burden of small businesses and tax administration procedures became less cumbersome and costly, mainly in bookkeeping and reporting. MSEs were eligible to use either simplified or general accounting procedures based on their preference.

---

[5] Welfare Improvement Strategy of Uzbekistan (2007) *Full Strategy Paper for 2008-2010* (Tashkent).

[6] Decree UP-1987 of the President of the Republic of Uzbekistan, "On further developing private enterprises and small businesses", 9 April 1998.

[7] Uzbekistan, Resolution #159 of the Cabinet of Ministers, "Procedures for Applying a Simplified System of Taxation for Micro-firms and Small businesses", 15 April 1998.

Despite the fundamental tax policy reforms instituted during the period 1992-1998, Uzbekistan scored 2 out of a possible 5 in an assessment of the degree of tax policy reform (Ebrill and Havrylyshyn 1999).[8]

The increasing number of small business and the complexity of the tax system created a need for qualified tax specialists. However, until the late 1990s, professional education for accountants and government employees was not available, and the system from licensing non-governmental educational institutions was costly and inflexible.

Phase 3 (2000-2004)

By the year 2000, the tax system of Uzbekistan had its established fiscal institution (the State Tax Committee) and regulatory framework (the Tax Code) as a result of the reforms implemented. The economy of Uzbekistan recovered after the separation from the Soviet Union and GDP was growing steadily. However, the overwhelming fiscal role of taxation created a high tax burden for the business sector, increased the shadow economy and suppressed investment. This was the time for new reforms directed towards enforcing the regulatory framework and stimulating the role of taxation through:

1. Reduction of the tax burden;

2. Further simplification of taxation procedures for small enterprises;

3. Simplification of tax administration.

High social security contributions and progressive income tax schedule

Mandatory social security fees, which have the same status as taxes, placed a substantial burden on MSEs. In 2004, businesses paid a consolidated social security contribution of 33 per cent of payroll. Revenue from the consolidated social security contribution is distributed among the extrabudgetary Pension Fund, the State Employment Fund and the Trade Unions Federation Council.[9] Contributions to these funds are levied on the same base[10] but administered separately. An entrepreneur has to transfer the amounts accrued to different accounts with the relevant agencies and submit separate tax calculations for each of them. This increases the administrative load on enterprises substantially.

In addition to consolidated social payment, large businesses also contribute a percentage of sales to the extrabudgetary Pension Fund.

---

[8] A staff team led by L. Ebrill and O. Havrylyshyn assessed the degree of policy reforms in a number of transition countries, using the five-point Likert scale, where 1 denotes very little appropriate market-oriented reform and 5 denotes a high degree of reform.

[9] From 1 January 2008, a consolidated social payment of 24 per cent is distributed among extrabudgetary funds as follows: Pension Fund – 23.5 per cent, state employment fund – 0.3 per cent and Trade Unions Federation Council – 0.2 per cent.

[10] The taxable base for the consolidated social contribution is the payroll.

Individuals in addition to paying personal income tax based on a progressive tax rate schedule,[11] pay contributions to the Pension Fund and dues to the Trade Unions Federation Council.[12]

As a result of the progressive personal income tax rate and high rates of social contributions, which are levied on payroll, neither employers nor employees are interested in formalizing the labour relationship. This restricts wage and salary increases as well as growth in the number of jobs, expands the shadow economy, deprives the government of revenues, and puts employees at a disadvantage. In a number of surveys, a substantial number of MSEs "solve" this issue by paying wages and salaries unofficially. In those cases, both the companies and the employees are breaking the law. However, high payroll deductions and personal income taxes make it customary to do so.

Double taxation, "tax on tax", and taxation of sales

A fundamental taxation principle—the one-time taxation of any taxable item—is not currently adhered to in Uzbekistan. For example, sales revenue is the basis not only for the single tax payment, in the case of the simplified taxation system, but also for mandatory payments to the pension fund, road fund, and education fund, in the case of the general tax regime.

The VAT on imports is calculated on a basis that includes the customs value, the excise tax and customs duties. This "tax on tax" is a heavy burden on the importer. The same applies to goods subject to excise tax produced in Uzbekistan.

Thus, even though the rates of taxes and other mandatory payments are low in comparison with neighbouring countries, the tax burden is actually hampering business development in Uzbekistan because the taxes (expenses, excise taxes and customs duties) are levied on the same taxable basis (International Finance Cooperation 2004).

Actions taken to reduce tax burden

Indirect taxes, which bring the highest revenues to the government budget, fulfil mainly the fiscal role of taxation, while direct taxes fulfil regulatory and stimulating roles. In order to strengthen the regulatory and stimulatory roles of taxation, the government reduced the tax rates of some direct taxes. Reduction of the tax burden is one of the instruments for stimulating local producers and developing entrepreneurial activities.

---

[11] From 1 January 2008: Lower band (up to six minimal wages) – 13 per cent, Middle band (6-10 minimal wages) – 18 per cent, Upper band (above 10 minimal wages) – 25 per cent. Minimal wage to 1 September 2008 = 25,040 UZS.

[12] Individuals contribute 1 per cent of their salary to extrabudgetary pension fund and 1 per cent to trade union fund.

Table 1. Changes in tax rates over the years 2000-2004
(Percentage)

	2000	2001	2002	2003	2004
Corporate Income Tax	31	26	24	20	18
Consolidated Social Payment	40	40	40	37.2	33
Individual Income Tax	Upper band-40	Upper band-36	Upper band-33	Upper band-32	Upper band-30
	Middle band-36	Middle band-25	Middle band-23	Middle band-22	Middle band-21
	Lower band-15	Lower band-12	Lower band-13	Lower band-13	Lower band-13

Source: Uzbekistan, Ministry of Finance, 2004.

Figure 3. Tax rate dynamics, 1996-2007

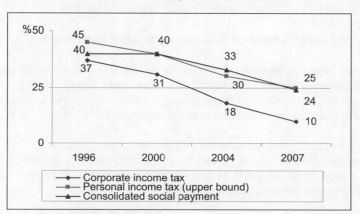

Source: Uzbekistan, Ministry of Finance, 2007.

It was expected that government losses due to the reduction of the tax burden would be partially compensated for by an increase in the tax base (i.e., through a reduction of tax exemptions) and in the voluntary compliance of taxpayers. Some models show that a reduction in the tax burden may result in reduced tax evasion and increase the voluntary compliance of taxpayers (Slemrod and Yizhaki 2000).

To further reduce the tax burden, give clear definitions of taxable bases and improve the cost accounting practices of enterprises, the Cabinet of Ministers of Uzbekistan on 15 October 2003 introduced changes and extended the list of tax-deductible items for enterprises.[13]

---

[13] Uzbekistan, Resolution #444 of Cabinet of Ministers, "On Improving Cost Accounting", 15 October 2003.

Taxation of MSEs

Despite the trend towards lower tax rates, they remained high in early 2000. In Uzbekistan, MSEs pay from 5 to 10 per cent of revenue, or 25 per cent of revenue less expenses as a single tax. In the Russian Federation, for example, for MSEs paying taxes under the simplified taxation system, the unified tax rate is 6 per cent of revenue or 15 per cent of revenue less expenses.[14]

The "simplified" taxation scheme for small enterprises is actually not, as it envisions that, for taxation purposes, gross revenues may not be lower than the cost of the product. According to this requirement, a small company is required to maintain cost accounting records on its products, which is one of the most complicated forms of accounting and requires a highly qualified accountant. Furthermore, for many small companies involved in providing services or works, there is no point in calculating costs, so they write off all their expenditures to operational costs (periodic costs), as this is simpler and more convenient. These requirements of tax legislation significantly complicate tax administration and increase costs for small businesses (International Finance Corporation 2004).

Actions taken to simplify taxation procedures for small enterprises

Changes were introduced to the criteria for identifying small businesses in 2003. According to the legislation of Uzbekistan, as of 1 January 2004,[15] there is no such term as "medium-sized business". Most medium-sized enterprises moved to small enterprises category and enjoyed a simplified order of taxation (annex 1).

From 1 July 2003, all wholesale/retail trade and catering enterprises (including MSEs) subject to the general tax regime moved to a simplified order of taxation and proposed payment of tax on gross revenues in lieu of all federal and local taxes and payments[16] (except trade, licensing and registration duties).

Furthermore, accounting and reporting procedures were simplified for all MSEs from 1 January 2004.[17]

One of the major achievements of phase 3 was creation of the Tax Academy – the first higher education institute specializing in preparing and retraining tax specialists – under the education centre of State Tax Committee.[18]

---

[14] Article #346.20 of the Tax Code of Russian Federation, available from http://www.russian-tax-code.com/

[15] Decree UP- 3305 of the President of Uzbekistan, "On Amending the Decree UP-1987 'On Measures to Promote the Further Development of Private Enterprises and Small Businesses' from April 9, 1998", 30 August 2003.

[16] Decree UP – 3270 of the President of Uzbekistan, "Measures regulating taxation of trading and catering enterprises", 30 June 2003.

[17] National Accounting Standard of the Republic of Uzbekistan #20, "About simplification of accounting and reporting procedures", 1 January 2004.

[18] Uzbekistan, Resolution #229 of the Cabinet of Ministers, "Preparing and retraining skilled personnel", 22 May 2003.

Phase 4 (2005 - present)

Tax reforms underwent a major overhaul in 2005 to eliminate certain features that were identified as having a negative impact on the growth of the private sector and the competitiveness of the national economy in the international arena. The most important of these are highlighted below.

Relatively high tax burden

In 2005, consolidated tax revenues made up 30.1 per cent of Uzbekistan's GDP.[19] Compared to developed countries, particularly the countries of Western Europe, this tax burden does not seem excessive. For example, in 2005, the average tax revenue in EU27 countries was 39.6 per cent, with the highest tax burdens in Denmark – 46.5 per cent and Ireland – 41.4 per cent (Finfacts 2008).

However, such a comparison is inappropriate. The tax burden of a country depends directly on its level of economic development: the more developed the economy, the greater the share of taxes in government expenditure (Vasilyeva et al. 2003). Hence, it is more sensible to compare Uzbekistan's tax burden of 30.1 per cent against that of other developing countries where GDP per capita is similar to the level of income in Uzbekistan, which rarely exceeds 20 to 25 per cent of GDP (for example, China and Thailand). During the years of phenomenal economic growth in China (1979–1996), the average tax burden was reduced from 36 per cent to 13 per cent and then rose gradually (after 18 years of record economic growth) to 20 per cent (Illarionov and Pivovarova 2002).

In 2004, the tax burden on Uzbek MSEs was an average of 20 per cent of revenue, which respondents considered excessive (International Finance Corporation 2004). In the opinion of entrepreneurs, the optimum tax rate for Uzbekistan would be 10 per cent of sales. High tax burdens reduce MSEs' competitiveness with foreign and local producers that have tax exemptions.[20]

MSEs that pay a single tax under the simplified system of taxation, in lieu of paying all other federal and local taxes, mandatory payments and duties, in reality end up paying, on average, five taxes (International Finance Corporation 2004. This is what contradicts the principles of a simplified system of taxation.

Actions taken to reduce the tax burden

On 20 June 2005, the Government of Uzbekistan introduced a single tax payment for MSEs operating in the manufacturing and service sectors of the economy.[21] This tax

---

[19] Tax revenue includes extrabudgetary funds.

[20] Having pursued an import-substituting strategy since 1997, the Government grants tax exceptions to enterprises that export goods and to enterprises targeted for production of import replacement products.

[21] Uzbekistan, "About Calculation and Payment of Single Tax Payment", 2 August 2005.

was intended to replace the existing single tax and mandatory payments to extrabudgetary funds.[22] The rates of single tax payment vary depending on the industry in which the MSE operates.

During the period from 1 July 2005 to 1 January 2007, three types of simplified systems of taxation for MSEs were in use:

1. Tax on Gross Revenues of Trade and Catering Enterprises – for wholesale/retail trade and catering enterprises (active as of 1 July 2003);[23]

2. Single Tax – for procurement, storage enterprises, enterprises providing services under commission contracts, brokerage enterprises (active as of 15 April 1998);

3. Single Tax Payment – for manufacturing and service enterprises (active as of 1 July 2005).

Tax rates, reporting and taxation bases were different for all three systems.[24] To reduce complexity and to unify the taxes of the simplified system of taxation, the Government of Uzbekistan combined all three taxes (single tax, single tax payment and tax on gross revenue) into one—the single tax payment[25] (annex 3).

Along with the introduction of a new tax for MSEs, some tax rates have been reduced since 2005, and the ecology tax was abolished in 2006.

Table 2. Changes in tax rates over the years 2005-2008
(Percentage)

	2005	2006	2007	2008
Corporate Income Tax	15	12	10	10
Consolidated Social Payment	31	25	24	24
Single Tax Payment	-	13	1	8
Individual income tax (upper band)	29	29	25	a

Source: Uzbekistan, Ministry of Finance, 2008.
a The lowest band expanded from 5 minimal wages up to 6.

---

[22] Single tax payment includes in itself mandatory payments to the extrabudgetary Pension Fund, Road Fund and School Fund.

[23] Decree UP – 3270 of the President of Uzbekistan, "About measures of regulating taxation of trading and catering enterprises", 30 June 2003.

[24] MSEs which paid tax on gross revenues during the period from 1 July 2003 to 1 July 2005 were required to submit monthly tax reports.

[25] Uzbekistan, Ministry of Finance, Resolution #26, "About Calculation and Payment of Single Tax Payment", 28 February 2007.

Some changes were introduced to the excise tax and the subsurface tax in 2004; the excise tax on energy carriers (such as gas, oil and coal) was replaced by a subsurface use tax.[26]

The reductions in tax rates, the introduction of new taxes and the abolishment of others changed the composition of taxes in government revenues. If in 2002, three taxes (individual income tax, VAT and excise tax) accounted for 62.8 per cent of all tax revenues, by 2006 this picture had changed; there were now four taxes (individual income tax, VAT, excise tax and subsurface use tax) constituting 70 per cent of all tax revenues.

As a result of broad government support directed to the expansion of MSEs' role in the economy of Uzbekistan and reduction of tax rates, the number of registered small businesses reached 422,300 in 2007 (Uzbekistan 2008a). According to the State Committee on Statistics, MSEs in 2007 account for 45.7 per cent of GDP and 72.3 per cent of total employment.

Figure 4.
Share of MSE as a percentage of GDP

Figure 5. Share of MSE as a percentage of employment

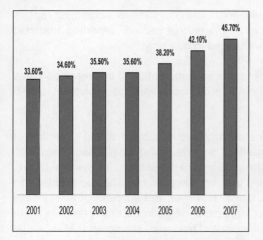

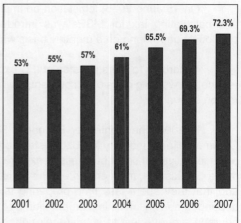

Source: Uzbekistan, State Committee on Statistics, 2008.

The share of MSEs in all sectors of the economy rose substantially in 2006 and 2007 compared with 2005.

---

[26] Uzbekistan, Resolution #610 of the Cabinet of Ministers, "About changes in rates of subsurface use tax", 28 December 2004.

Table 3. Share of MSE in selected sectors of economy
(Percentage)

	Industry	Agriculture	Investments in equity	Construction	Trade	Services (paid)
2005	9.4	85.7	22.1	48.2	43.7	52.5
2006	10.0	93.9	25.2	51.0	45.7	50.8
2007	12.9	97.5	19.9	53.7	47.2	50.5

Source: State Committee on Statistics of the Republic of Uzbekistan, 2008.

Changes introduced to tax administration

On 14 June 2005, a presidential decree was introduced on improving the legal protection of businesses.[27] This decree restricted excessive intervention by controlling authorities in the business operations of MSEs.

On 15 June 2005, legislation on improvements to the system for submitting reports and calculating tax for MSEs was introduced.[28] Under this decree, reporting that had previously been done on a monthly basis was changed to quarterly.

According to the estimates of IFC experts, the implementation of this resolution may reduce the working days of accountants by about 2 million days, which is equivalent to $6.5 million annually.[29]

In 2005, the Center for Economic Research, with the support of the Chamber of Commerce and Industry of Uzbekistan, organized several round-table discussions with representatives of small business to explore the problems of the existing tax system. During those discussions, most entrepreneurs admitted that reporting had become less problematic and that they spent less time preparing tax forms. However, the success of this novelty depended heavily on its implementation by tax inspectors. Sometimes, entrepreneurs spent hours in a queue just to submit their financial reports. There was still some evidence that tax inspectors rejected documents on the grounds of an incorrect format or for some other mundane detail. But small "incentives" could fix the problem.

---

[27] Uzbekistan, Resolution #610 of the Cabinet of Ministers, "About changes in rates of subsurface use tax", 28 December 2004. Decree UP-3619 of the President of Uzbekistan, "On Further Improving the System of Legal Protection of Businesses", 14 June 2005.

[28] Resolution PP-100 of the President of Uzbekistan, "On Improving the System of Business Reporting and Raising Penalty for Illegal Demand", 15 June 2005.

[29] This represents the amount of accountants' fees saved as a result of the reduction in the frequency of submissions.

On 24 June 2005, legislation was introduced to reduce the financial penalties and an exemption for minor, unintentional, first-time violations.[30]

The biggest threat for entrepreneurs is prosecution. The smallest breach of rules, even when an entrepreneur admits his guilt and is ready to pay fines, might result in the case being handed over to prosecutors.

On 5 October 2005, a presidential decree was issued to reduce the number of inspections further.[31]

A survey conducted by IFC in January and February 2006 revealed that the average number of annual inspections had fallen from 1.2 in 2005 to 0.9 in 2004.[32] According to the above-mentioned decree, the financial-economic activities of enterprises can only be assessed by tax authorities.[33] Furthermore, sanctions such as stopping or closing down the operational activities of an enterprise, cancelling licences or permits, or tying up money can be done only through the courts. This decree may save MSEs $21 million annually.

Despite government measures directed towards reducing the number of inspections, the emphasis of inspections is still on exposing violations and imposing penalties rather than on assisting entrepreneurs in avoiding violations and addressing shortcomings.

The system of selecting enterprises for inspection is not transparent. As a result, businesses with higher cash turnover are inspected more frequently than those that can cause potentially more danger to public health, the environment, or the country's economy.

Flaws in the regulatory framework

The steadiness of small businesses greatly depends on the stability of tax legislation. Flaws in the regulatory framework might be fatal for MSEs—entrepreneurs simply cannot keep up with the pace of changes, and the first serious tax mistake usually ends in the termination of the entrepreneur's business.

The Tax Code adopted on 1 January 1998 was produced quickly and had many weaknesses. More than 310 amendments had to be made over time. In addition, it was very condensed and required many normative acts (about 1,300) before it could be implemented. This hyperactive lawmaking had as a major consequence the poor integration and misinterpretation of by-laws and normative acts, which frequently contradicted each

---

[30] Decree UP-3622 of the President of Uzbekistan, "On Liberalizing Financial Liability of Businesses for Economic Violations", 24 June 2005.

[31] Decree UP-3665 of the President of Uzbekistan, "On Further Reducing and Improving the System of Inspections of Businesses", 5 October 2005.

[32] In 2001, the average number of annual inspections per enterprise was 6.2; in 2002 it was 4.2; and in 2003, it was 1.9.

[33] Over 40 government organizations have authority to inspect business enterprises in Uzbekistan.

other. As a result, tax legislation became unsystematic, non-transparent and burdensome to businesspeople.

The findings of an entrepreneurial survey (Center for Economic Research 2006) indicated the difficulty of running a successful business within the existing regulatory framework: 68.5 per cent of respondents expressed concern with the complexities and contradictions of legislation and 57.2 per cent highlighted problems of non-transparency in the tax system.

Given the unpredictability of tax liability, companies cannot adequately manage their cash flow or plan business development. Moreover, the frequent changes in taxation requirements, of which businesses are not made aware, prevent MSEs from complying with tax legislation.

Ambiguous and inconsistent legislative norms lead to tax evasion and corruption among tax officials.

Changes introduced to stabilize the regulatory framework

On 1 January 2008, the new edition of the Tax Code was adopted. It unifies and streamlines tax legislation, particularly with regard to tax administration; it also replaces normative acts, decrees and by-laws of the former tax system. It sets forth the whole system of taxes and dues, including customs duties, without reference to additional regulatory acts encompassing the whole range of tax relations both substantive and procedural.

More than 7,000 suggestions of local entrepreneurs[34] were taken into consideration in preparing the new edition of the Tax Code.

According to the State Committee on Statistics, changes in the new edition of the Tax Code increased government revenue from the corporate income tax to 42.6 per cent and from the single tax payment to 36.0 per cent in the first six months of 2008 compared with the same period the previous year (Uzbekistan 2008).

III. METHODOLOGY

This report is based on the results of a survey undertaken in July and August of 2008. On-site standardized interviews were conducted with 30 representatives of MSEs in five regions of Uzbekistan.

---

[34] The Chamber of Commerce and Industry created a special Internet forum to communicate with representatives of the business sector about the new edition of Tax Code.

Respondents were classified into micro-firms and small businesses according to the legislation of Uzbekistan that came into effect as of 1 January 2004.[35] In 2008, the simplified order of taxation envisages the payment of one of the following:[36]

1. *Single Tax Payment*. MSEs may opt for the application of the single tax payment in lieu of paying all other federal and local taxes, mandatory payments and duties (except of excise tax, VAT, customs duties in respect of imports and consolidated social payment).

2. *Single Land Tax*. Agricultural enterprises (agricultural producers) are subject to a single land tax in lieu of all federal and local taxes (except for excise taxes and social payments). The taxable base is the land area owned, used or rented by the taxpayer.

3. *Fixed Tax*. Legal entities and individuals involved in certain entrepreneurial activities are subject to a fixed tax payable on the basis of fixed rates. The list of activities subject to the fixed tax includes provision of hairstyling services, billiards, rent/sale of video and audiotapes, catering (by individuals only) and computer games.

In this paper, only MSEs making the single tax payment are analysed.

Tax reforms that took place during the fourth phase of Uzbek tax system development were mainly targeted on providing measures for further developing small businesses; therefore, this research aims to study the influence of recent tax reforms on the prosperity of local micro-firms and small businesses.[37] To derive accurate results, MSEs established in 2005 and earlier will form the population of the research.

Sample Selection

The five regions of Uzbekistan chosen to conduct interviews are: Andijan, Samarkand, Tashkent, the Republic of Karakalpakstan and Tashkent City. Andijan, Samarkand and Tashkent regions are the most densely populated regions of Uzbekistan and they have the highest growth rates among the regional economies.[38] The Republic of Karakalpakstan, an autonomous Uzbek republic, has the largest territory among the 14 administrative

---

[35] Decree UP- 3305 of the President of Uzbekistan, "On Amending the Decree UP-1987 'On Measures to Promote the Further Development of Private Enterprises and Small Businesses' from April 9, 1998", 30 August 2003.

[36] Revised Edition of Tax Code 2008.

[37] Changes introduced in the new edition of the Tax Code, in particular the reduction in the rate of the single tax payment from 10 per cent to 8 per cent, are outside the scope of this research, mainly because they are too recent.

[38] According to the Socio-Economic Indicators for 2007 of the State Committee on Statistics, in the Tashkent region, the gross regional product in 2007 rose by 16.8 per cent, in Samarkand by 11.6 per cent, and in Andijan by 10.5 per cent (the average in Uzbekistan is 9.5 per cent).

subdivisions of the country but a relatively low economic growth rate. Tashkent is an independent city and the capital of Uzbekistan.

The scope of the research encompassed all registered MSEs. The sample for research was randomly selected from the annually renewed database of the Chamber of Commerce and Industry, based on the following criteria:

1. Regions in which MSEs operate;

2. Economic sectors in which MSEs are engaged.

Three sectors of the economy were observed in the current research:

*   Manufacturing

*   Wholesale/retail sale and catering enterprises

*   Service sector

MSEs operating in these three sectors of the economy have different tax burdens for the following reasons:

(a) The retail sale of certain types of products—for example, alcohol, tobacco products, and articles of jewellery containing precious metals or stones—is subject to local taxes/fees, and enterprises engaging in such activities are required to pay those local taxes in addition to making the single tax payment, which goes to the federal coffers;

(b) enterprises usually pay excise tax and customs duties and even VAT when they import goods. The same is true for manufacturing enterprises when they import components or raw materials for their production process;

(c) Service enterprises usually make only a single tax payment.

Calculating the Tax Burden of Enterprises

Within the framework of the current research, the tax burden of enterprises was calculated using the following formula:

$$TaxBurden = \frac{TaxPayments}{Gross\ Revenue} \times 100\%$$

where: *Tax Payments* include all tax payments made by an enterprise, withholding tax on dividends, interest and brokerage fees;

Gross Revenue includes revenue from the sale of goods (rendering services) and other revenues, including indirect taxes.

The larger the figure, the higher the tax burden of an enterprise.

IV. PRESENTATION OF FINDINGS

Main characteristics of respondents

The average age of respondents was 42 years. Most firms are started by and operated by men (68 per cent). Managing the demands of both work and family is a continuing challenge for Uzbek female entrepreneurs, and in the conflict between work and family roles, Uzbek women are inclined more towards fulfilling their family roles. Promoting gender equality is an integral element of human development, and social welfare will be enhanced as the economic independence of women is furthered through equal opportunities to employment and entrepreneurship, particularly in rural areas (Welfare Improvement Strategy of Uzbekistan 2007). Uzbek women have much undiscovered potential which, given the right opportunities and conditions, could increase the number of MSEs in Uzbekistan.

Main characteristics of business

Most of the enterprises interviewed were micro-firms (63.66 per cent) with an average of 7.3 employees in 2005. By 2007, the average number of employees had reached 8.7, which represents a growth rate of 16 per cent over three years.

Evaluation of the current tax environment

Tax system

The vast majority (93.33 per cent) of the MSEs observed pay taxes according to the simplified order of taxation. The average tax burden for 30 interviewed enterprises was 14.9 per cent, with the highest being 18.3 per cent and the lowest 5.6 per cent.

Changes in the enterprise as a result of the transition to a single tax payment

A total of 69 per cent of respondents thought that moving to a single tax payment had made tax reporting less problematic, 58 per cent thought the tax burden had been reduced, and 35 per cent thought there had been no change since the move to a single tax payment.

Moving to a single tax payment influenced mainly wholesale/retail sale and catering enterprises, which were subject to tax on their gross profits, with monthly reporting obligations to tax agencies.

Factors influencing the business activities of MSEs

As can be seen from figure 6, business activity is most negatively influenced by the instability of tax legislation (89 per cent), followed by the incompetence of tax inspectors (78 per cent) and tax inspections (65 per cent).

A survey of entrepreneurs held in April and May 2006 by the Center for Economic Research gave similar results: 54.4 per cent of respondents thought it was impossible to operate in Uzbekistan without breaking the law.

Figure 6. Factors hindering the business activities of MSEs

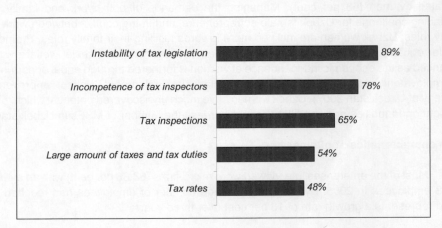

Tax administration

Reporting

According to 65 per cent of respondents, there is no difference in the level of difficulty of the tax reporting process in 2006 and in 2007; 45 per cent of MSE representatives thought that the tax reporting procedure in 2007 was just as difficult as in 2006, while the rest—55 per cent—thought that the tax reporting procedure in 2007 was the same as in 2006.

Inspections

Every MSE, on average, provided 1.5 times additional information or documents to tax authorities during the period under observation. Additional documents most often were requested from retail trade and public catering enterprises. There was an extreme case concerning a small enterprise operating in the services sector which was asked to provide additional information and documents to the State Tax Committee every single month!

It should be pointed out there are no restrictions on the State Tax Agency's legal right to demand additional information.[39] This increases the administrative burden on the entrepreneurs, who must then prepare and submit that information.

Most tax inspections (95 per cent), both scheduled and unscheduled, were conducted in MSEs that operate in the wholesale/retail trade and catering sectors of the economy.

Bribes

Every second respondent confessed that he/she paid money or bribed government officials to find a solution to a problem or to settle down a question related to business.

When bribery is involved, in 23.8 per cent of cases, it happens during tax inspections.

Violations of MSEs' rights

In cases where the rights of MSEs were violated, 28.6 per cent of entrepreneurs sought help from executive courts and advocates.

Tax reform

A total of 62 per cent of respondents were familiar with *all* the changes that had taken place in tax legislation related to small businesses during the period 2005-2007. And 38 per cent of respondents were familiar with *some* of the changes in the tax regulations.

The reduction of the single tax payment rate from 13 per cent to 10 per cent in 2007 created additional resources for MSEs to invest or expand their production, according to 47.3 per cent of respondents.

Self-evaluation of well-being

Respondents were asked twice to evaluate their well-being. The first time, they were asked to give a number, on a scale of 1 to 10, where 1 is the lowest level of income and 10 the highest. The weighted average score for MSEs interviewed was 4.8.

The second time, respondents were requested to describe their financial situation before they started their business and currently, using the five-point Likert scale (1 – very bad, 2 – bad, 3 – satisfactory, 4 – good and 5 – very good). According to the results of the survey, the material well-being of entrepreneurs improved from 2.88 to 3.76.

---

[39] According to Article 5 of Law 474-1 of Uzbekistan, "On the State Taxation Service", 29 August 1997, tax agencies, within their competence, have the right to obtain from legal entities and individuals information, references, documents, and copies of documents relating to the taxpayer's activity.

Despite the observed improvement of welfare, entrepreneurs spent 57.5 per cent of their net profit from the business on personal and family consumption, leaving only 25.4 per cent of profit for reinvestment purposes and 8.6 per cent for savings.

Evaluation of business and the business environment

Respondents were asked to evaluate the state of their business and the business environment using the five-point Likert scale:

- As at the end of 2007;

- As at the base year, 2005, when the start was given to major tax reform to further support entrepreneurship and small business development.

- As can be seen from table 3, a slight improvement of +0.1 and +0.25 was observed in both the state of business and the business environment as at the end of 2007.

Table 4. Evaluation of the state of business and business environment, 2005 and 2007

State of business		Business environment	
2005	2007	2005	2007
3.05	3.15	2.55	2.7

V. RECOMMENDATIONS

Inspections

Establishing risk-based audits

To address the issues related to the way enterprises are selected for tax inspections, it is necessary to eliminate the subjectivity of the selection process. International experience shows that the most effective method of selecting enterprises for inspection is the one based on an analysis of the potential risks involved in the business activity. Under this method, the selection and the frequency of inspection depend on the extent of the potential danger that the operation of the business may pose to public health, the environment or the country's economy.

Under the current tax inspection system, the additional revenue collected as a result of tax audits is only 1.24 times the cost of maintaining a tax inspector. By comparison, in Kazakhstan it is 4.6 times and in the Russian Federation 5.7 times (Soliev et al. 2007).

In the United States, implementing the Discriminant Function System (DIF), a software programme that selects taxpayers for inspection on the basis of the tax declaration forms submitted, brought the number of unsuccessful inspections (i.e. those that brought no additional tax revenue to the federal budget) down from 46 per cent in 1969 to 15 per cent in 1992.[40]

According to initial calculations, the development and implementation of the risk-analysis system in Uzbekistan will require 7 billion sums.[41] In exchange, Uzbekistan would benefit from the following:

(a) Improved efficiency of resource distribution at tax inspectorates. This is especially true in the case of Uzbekistan, where the conditions associated with liberalizing the national economy and creating a more favourable business environment are rapidly driving up the number of MSEs. For example, during the last three years, the number of registered small enterprises increased from 237,502 to 346,062 (Uzbekistan 2008). According to expert estimations, the workload per tax inspector will increase by more than 45 per cent within three years. An additional 300 tax inspectors would need to be recruited in order to keep up with the current workload. By 2011, salaries alone would cost the government 1.3 billion sums (Soliev et al. 2007). If, on the other hand, the current number of tax inspectors and the existing mechanisms of tax control are retained, the scope of inspections will be reduced by 30 per cent, with a corresponding reduction in effectiveness;

(b) Reduced pressure on successful, law-abiding enterprises and the creation of an additional incentive for entrepreneurs to comply with legal requirements, because the frequency of inspections will depend on their compliance with established rules and standards;

(c) Reduced potential for officials at various levels to abuse their positions by using inspections to punish entrepreneurs;

Introduction of distance control

On-site inspections should be replaced by off-site inspections ("cameral inspections") whereby tax officials scrutinize all documents from their offices. Introducing distance audits in Uzbekistan will allow MSEs to carry out their normal operations and reduce the number of extortion cases during the audit process.

---

[40] Ibid.

[41] This calculation was made by a team of United Nations experts in Uzbekistan in connection with a project on improving tax administration in Uzbekistan. On the basis of the Central Bank of Uzbekistan's exchange rate on 9 September 2008 (1 United States dollar = 1,324.6 Uzbek sums), 7 billion sums is equivalent to $5,284,614.

The new edition of the Tax Code has a special section governing cameral inspections, the purpose of which is to audit taxpayer compliance, detect tax violations, and make a demand for the unpaid amount of taxes. The results of cameral inspections can serve as criteria for the selection of enterprises for tax inspections.

Reporting

Electronic submission of reports

Information and communications technology should be used extensively in the reforms. International practices illustrate greater efficiency in administration and fewer opportunities for corruption and abuse in governance when electronic systems and technologies are used. The digitalization of administrative processes is the next logical step after unification and harmonization of procedures.

The computerization of reporting processes will reduce time for both taxpayers and tax authorities. But most importantly, it will reduce the significance of the human factor in assessing reports, i.e., it will increase objectivity and the transparency of the work of tax authorities.[42]

Tax authorities have already started piloting the electronic submission of tax forms in Tashkent City and Tashkent region. A successful conclusion of the pilot test will pave the way for nationwide e-submission of tax reports.

The benefits of computerizing reporting processes are obvious, but are Uzbek MSEs ready for this change? A survey of entrepreneurs held in April and May 2006 by the Center for Economic Research has revealed a very low rate of computerization in domestic companies—only 36 per cent of MSEs have at least one computer. The results were even worse for micro-firms and enterprises in the Djizakh, Sirdarya and Khorezm regions of Uzbekistan. MSEs operating in the agriculture, public catering and medical services sectors were the least equipped with computers. With computerization as well as the computer literacy of local MSEs at such a low level, implementing compulsory e-submission practices might be perceived by MSEs as another obstacle to their activities. Yet, 81.1 per cent of respondents gave a positive answer to the question: "If there was an opportunity, would you submit tax reports through the Internet?" Step-by-step implementation of e-submission practices combined with continuous training of MSEs will improve existing tax reporting practices.

---

[42] The New Technologies Scientific and Information Center, with financial support from UNDP in Uzbekistan, is developing a software package entitled "Receipts and Processing of Tax Returns and Taxpayer Financial Reporting for Generating Statistical Reports by State Tax Service Bodies" for the State Tax Committee of Uzbekistan. The objective of this development is to streamline the submission of financial reports and tax returns and to reduce the impact of subjective factors (such as errors by taxpayers and official abuse) on this process. The software package enables tax returns to be submitted through the Internet, thereby reducing the amount of time spent waiting in line during tax inspections.

Creating dedicated administrative structures in the national tax committee

Creating dedicated administrative structures in the national tax committee will help to address the specific needs of small businesses and enable the tax administration to combat tax evasion in the MSE community efficiently (International Finance Corporation 2005a).

Offering specific service and information programmes to the MSE community

MSEs should know and understand their rights and obligations. Research conducted by PricewaterhouseCoopers in 2006 showed that only 41 per cent of small taxpayers in OECD countries were aware of incentives and tax relief opportunities, while only 11 per cent actually used them (PricewaterhouseCoopers 2007b). In the case of Uzbekistan's small taxpayers, these figures are likely to be even lower. If tax authorities could design and offer specific information material and training courses, relations between them and MSEs could improve

Reduction of tax burden

In comparison with international practice, the tax burden in Uzbekistan is not high. The problem is that some taxes are too high. For example, an employee who receives an after-tax salary of 100,000 sums costs the enterprise 200,000. Income tax in combination with pension payments increases the tax burden of an enterprise. Under these circumstances, both employer and employee may see a benefit in declaring lower salaries in official documents.

The most efficient stimulus for the developing Uzbek economy is the reduction of the consolidated social payment rate and the rate of individual income tax (Saidova et al. 2006). Reducing these tax rates will encourage an increase in payroll and declared revenues.

At the same time, the sensitivity of government revenues to the changes in tax rates requires the additional measures of improving tax collection and limiting informal turnover of financial assets.

Setting additional criteria for MSE classification

The current classification of MSEs (based on head count) puts two enterprises with different levels of turnover in one group. Additional criteria—for example, average annual turnover combined with the classification of the type of activity—should be introduced so as to allow more accurate targeting of MSEs.

Human resources

The Government of Uzbekistan has advanced considerably in developing human resources since its independence in 1991. Creating, in 2003, the first higher education institute dedicated to preparing and retraining tax specialists and abandoning the notion that "taxation is an accountant's job" could serve as a proof of this progress. Nevertheless, the qualifications of staff in the tax and customs authorities still leave much to be desired. Both procedural and technical reforms will work only if they are supported by adequately qualified staff. Improving the skills of civil servants will require a major effort, but it is essential if they are to be empowered to meet the objectives of the reforms.

According to the results of a UNDP survey in 2007, the majority of taxpayers complain about the low level of professional knowledge of tax authorities, unsatisfactory communication skills and lack of willingness to teach novices in the tax system. On the other hand, a survey conducted among tax officers detected a lack of economic as well as legal and business accounting knowledge among most tax inspectors.

The role of international organizations is crucial in improving the qualifications of the tax authorities. Such organizations as USAID and the Japan International Cooperation Center (JICE) have organized foreign internship programmes for the civil servants of Uzbekistan. Since 2008, UNDP, in cooperation with IFC, OSCE and OECD, has been holding short-term courses for tax authorities on innovations in tax legislation, new methods of tax control, and the specifics of taxation of particular activities.

VI. CONCLUSION

The Government of Uzbekistan attaches great importance to the development of MSEs and has integrated small business development issues into its national strategic plan for economic and social development. In order to promote the development of MSEs, the Government has gradually amended relevant legislation and launched a series of policies and initiatives.

One of the tools that can have a favourable influence on the private sector development is the tax system. In Uzbekistan, the taxation system has undergone significant reforms since independence, but most of the changes were directed towards enforcing the fiscal role of taxation and stabilizing government revenues.

Effective tax reform cannot be accomplished in isolation from the current capabilities of the tax administration systems or the taxpayers' culture. The Government of Uzbekistan focuses primarily on modernizing tax policies and relegates tax administration and taxpayer compliance issues to a remote second place.

The high tax burden on businesses led to high rates of tax evasion. To improve the country's economic situation, the Government started to reduce tax rates, hoping through this to increase taxpayer compliance. However, the factors leading to high compliance of MSEs involve not only a low tax burden but also the simplicity of the tax administration from the taxpayer's point of view. A correctly constructed tax administration will contribute greatly towards bringing the informal economy into the tax net.

The biggest challenge for tax administrations in CIS countries remains that of transforming into more market-friendly institutions stressing self-assessment, taxpayer services and enforcement—and Uzbekistan is no exception. A broadly accepted principle in tax administration is that the ultimate goal of any tax administration is to promote voluntary compliance. The Government should encourage voluntary taxpayer compliance. This is the next step in the reform of the tax system in Uzbekistan: the government helps the taxpayer to make tax assessments through the use of highly credible and effective enforcement mechanisms, via audits and legal actions, not only to collect what is due but also to deter any abuse of greater freedoms granted (Lorie 2003).

To be effective and successful, tax reform needs to be accompanied by institutional and structural reform throughout the economy. In particular, institutional reform in areas complementary to fiscal reform, such as accounting, banking and foreign exchange, are of crucial importance to Uzbekistan.

Furthermore, the role of human resources—highly skilled tax officials—cannot be overemphasized in a successful tax reform. The Government of Uzbekistan needs to focus its attention on further development of human resources by creating non-governmental educational institutes and organizing professional training for both tax authorities and MSEs in order to implement its tax reforms effectively and efficiently.

Research has shown that changes in tax rates and tax administration influence the prosperity of entrepreneurs. In three years, both the prosperity of entrepreneurs and the business environment have improved.

The Government of Uzbekistan should continue the policy of reducing the tax burden aimed at maintaining the competitiveness of local MSEs as well as improving the tax and customs administration systems.

The findings of the present paper can, to certain extent, apply to other Central Asian countries and serve as an initial overview of the fiscal and socio-economic situation of neighbouring republics, since they have many things in common: roots, cultural values, traditions and the consequences of the collapse of the Soviet Union.

REFERENCES

Center for Economic Research (2006). *Entrepreneurs of Uzbekistan: problems, opinions, social picture* (Social Research, Tashkent, Uzbekistan).

Ebrill, L. and O. Havrylyshyn (1999). "Tax reform in the Baltics, Russia, and other countries of the former Soviet Union", Occasional Paper No. 182 (Washington, D.C., International Monetary Fund).

Finfacts, Ireland's Business and Finance Portal (2008), accessed from http://www.finfacts.com/ irelandbusinessnews/publish/article_1011514.shtml, on 25/08/2008].

Gemayel, E. and D. Grigorian (2005). *"How tight is too tight? A look at welfare implications of distortionary policies in Uzbekistan"* Working Paper WP/05/239 (Washington, D.C., International Monetary Fund).

Illarionov, A. and N. Pivovarova (2002). "The size of the government and economic growth". *Vosposi Ekonomiki*, 9, pp. 40-41.

International Finance Corporation (2004). *Business Environment in Uzbekistan as Seen by Small and Medium Enterprises* (Survey, Tashkent, Uzbekistan).

International Finance Corporation (2005a). *Business Environment in Uzbekistan as Seen by Small and Medium Enterprises* (Survey, Tashkent, Uzbekistan).

International Finance Corporation (2005b). *Doing Business in 2005: Removing Obstacles to Growth* (The World Bank Project).

International Finance Corporation (2007a). *Designing a Tax System for Micro and Small Businesses: A guide to practitioners* (Washington D.C.).

International Finance Corporation (2007b). *Tax Administrations and Small and Medium Enterprises (SMEs) in Developing Countries* (Washington D.C.).

International Monetary Fund (1991). *A Study of Soviet Economy* (IMF, World Bank, OECD, and EBRD).

International Monetary Fund (2000). "Republic of Uzbekistan: Recent economic developments". Staff Country Report No. 00/36 (Washington, D.C., International Monetary Fund).

International Tax and Investment Center (2008). accessed from http://www.iticnet.org/publications/ Default.htm, on 20 August 2008.

Karimov, I. (2008). *Social-Economic Results of the Year 2007 and Priority Courses of Economic Reforms of the Year 2008.* Speech by the President of Uzbekistan, 8 August.

Kornai, J. (1997). *Struggle and Hope, Essays on Stabilization and Reform in a Post-Socialist Economy* (Edward Elgar Publishing Limited: Northampton, Massachusetts, pp. 239-254).

Lorie, H. (2003). "Priorities for further fiscal reforms in the Commonwealth of Independent States, Working Paper WP/03/209 (Washington, D.C., International Monetary Fund).

Martinez-Vazquez, J. and R. McNab (2003). "The tax reform experiment in transitional countries" Working Paper 00-1 (Georgia State University, Andrew Young School of Policy Studies, International Studies Program).

McLiesh, C. and R. Ramalho (2007). *Paying Taxes: The global picture.* (PricewaterhouseCoopers, World Bank).

PricewaterhouseCoopers (2007a). *Business and Investment Guide.* (Uzbekistan).

PricewaterhouseCoopers (2007b). *Paying Taxes: The global picture* (PricewaterhouseCoopers, World Bank).

Russian Federation (2008). *Tax Code of the Russian Federation,* accessed from http://www.russian-tax-code.com/, on 22 August 2008.

Saidova, G., Y. Fayzullayeva, K. Inomhodjaeva, A. Shapavatova, and S. Chepel (2006). "Modeling influence of tax rates changes on macroeconomic indicators" Working Paper (UNDP in Uzbekistan, Project on Tax System Reforms and Development of New Revised Tax Code).

Slemrod, J. and S. Yizhaki (2000). "Tax avoidance, evasion and administration", Research Working Paper No.7473 (National Bureau of Economic Research).

Soliev, N., R. Ahmedgariev, N. Vahabov, U. Nabiev, and N. Shmakova, (2007). "Perspectives of implementing risk-analysis to tax audit system in Uzbekistan", Working Paper (UNDP in Uzbekistan, Project on Improving Tax Administration in Uzbekistan).

Tanzi, V. and G. Tsibouris (2000). "Fiscal reform over ten years of transition, Working Paper WP/00/113 (Washington, D.C., International Monetary Fund).

Tuchkova, Z. (2008). "On the basis of new Tax Code – transformation of current tax system", *UzAhborot,* 13 March 2008).

Uzbekistan (2007). *Socio-Economic Results of the Year 2007* (Tashkent, State Committee on Statistics of the Republic of Uzbekistan).

Uzbekistan (2008a). *Socio-Economic Results of the First Half of the Year 2008* (Tashkent, State Committee on Statistics of the Republic ofUzbekistan).

Uzbekistan (2008b). *Tax Code of the Republic of Uzbekistan* 2008 (Tashkent, Norma).

Vasilyeva, A., E. Gurvich, and V. Subbotin (2003). "Economical analysis of tax reforms", *Questions of Economy,* Issue 6.

Welfare Improvement Strategy of Uzbekistan (2007). *Full Strategy Paper for 2008-2010* (Tashkent, Uzbekistan).

World Bank (2000). *World Development Indicators* (Washington, D.C., World Bank).

World Bank Group (2007). *Designing a Tax System for Micro and Small Businesses, A Guide to Practitioners* (The World Bank Group in collaboration with DFID).

Decrees and resolutions

1. Law 474-1 of the Republic of Uzbekistan, "On the State Taxation Service", 29 August 29 1997.

2. National Accounting Standard of the Republic of Uzbekistan #20, "About simplification of accounting and reporting procedures", 1 January 2004

3. National Accounting Standards of the Republic of Uzbekistan, Paragraph 5.9 "On the Procedures for Simplified Accounting and Reporting by MSEs", registered by the Ministry of Justice on 24 January 2000, #879.

4. Decree UP-1987 of President of the Republic of Uzbekistan, "On Further Developing Private Enterprises and Small Businesses" 9 April 1998.

5. Decree UP- 3305 of the President of the Republic of Uzbekistan "On Amending the Decree UP-1987 'On Measures to Promote the Further Development of Private Enterprises and Small Businesses' from April 9, 1998", 30 August 2003.

6. Decree UP – 3270 of the President of the Republic of Uzbekistan, "About measures of regulating taxation of trading and catering enterprises", 30 June 2003.

7. Decree UP-3619 of the President of the Republic of Uzbekistan, "On Further Improving the System of Legal Protection of Businesses", 14 June 2005.

8. Decree UP-3620 of the President of the Republic of Uzbekistan, "On Additional Incentives for the Development of Micro-firms and Small Businesses", 20 June 2005.

9. Decree UP-3622 of the President of the Republic of Uzbekistan, "On Liberalizing Financial Liability of Businesses for Economic violations", 24 June 2005.

10. Decree UP-3665 of the President of the Republic of Uzbekistan, "On Further Reducing and Improving the System of Inspections of Businesses", 5 October 2005.

11. Resolution PP-24 of the President of the Republic of Uzbekistan, "On the Program for Implementing the Objectives and Tasks of Democratizing and Renewing Society, and Reforming and Modernizing the Country", 10 March 2005.

12. Resolution PP-56 of the President of the Republic of Uzbekistan, "On Further Reforming and Liberalizing the Banking System", 15 April 2006.

13. Resolution PP-100 of the President of the Republic of Uzbekistan, "On Improving the System of Business Reporting and Raising Penalty for Illegal Demand", 15 June 2005.

14. Resolution PP-147 of the President of the Republic of Uzbekistan, "On Guarantees of Unimpeded Provision of Cash Payments from Bank Deposits", 5 August 2005.

15. Resolution PP-186 of the President of the Republic of Uzbekistan, "On Reducing the Types and Simplifying Permit Procedures for Entrepreneurial Activity", 21 September 2005.

16. Resolution #159 of the Cabinet of Ministers of the Republic of Uzbekistan, "Procedures of Applying Simplified System of Taxation for Micro-firms and Small businesses", 15 April 1998.

17. Resolution #65 of the Cabinet of Ministers of the Republic of Uzbekistan, "On Measures to Reduce and Put in Order Reporting by Small Enterprises", 23 February 2000.

18. Resolution #347 of the Cabinet of Ministers of the Republic of Uzbekistan, "On Improving the System for Registering Entrepreneurial Entities", 22 August 2001.

19. Resolution #229 of the Cabinet of Ministers of the Republic of Uzbekistan, "Preparing and retraining skilled personnel", 22 May 2003.

20. Resolution #357 of the Cabinet of Ministers of the Republic of Uzbekistan, "On Radically Improving the System of Registration Procedures in Establishing Business", 20 August 2003.

21. Resolution #444 of Cabinet of Ministers of the Republic of Uzbekistan, "On Improving Cost Accounting" 15 October 2003

22. Resolution #610 of the Cabinet of Ministers of the Republic of Uzbekistan, "About changes in tax rates of subsurface use tax", 28 December 2004.

23. Resolution #26 of Ministry of Finance of the Republic of Uzbekistan, "About Calculation and Payment of Single Tax Payment", 28 February 2007.

24. Resolution #69 of Minister of Finance of the Republic of Uzbekistan, "About Calculation and Payment of Single Tax Payment", 2 August 2005.

ANNEX I

DEFINITION OF MSEs ACCORDING TO UZBEK LEGISLATION

Small and Medium Enterprises (prior to 1 January 2004)	Micro and Small Enterprises (after 1 January 2004)
1. INDIVIDUAL ENTREPRENEURS	**1. INDIVIDUAL ENTREPRENEURS**
2. Micro-firms with an average annual number of employees not exceeding:	**2. Micro-firms with an average annual number of employees not exceeding:**
10 – in manufacturing sectors;	*20 – in manufacturing sectors;*
5 - in services and other non-manufacturing sectors;	*10 - in services and other non-manufacturing sectors;*
5 - in trade.	*5 - in wholesale and retail trade and public catering.*
3. Small enterprises with an average annual number of employees not exceeding:	**3. Small enterprises with an average annual number of employees not exceeding:**
40 – in industry;	*100 – in food, light industry, metal work and instrument-making, woodworking, furniture industry and construction materials;*
20 – in agriculture and other manufacturing sectors;	*50 – in mechanical engineering, metallurgy, fuel and energy, and chemicals;*
20 – in construction;	*50 – in agriculture and other industrial and manufacturing sectors;*
10 – in science, research services; retail trade and other non-manufacturing sectors;	*50 – in construction;*
4. Medium enterprises with an average annual number of employees not exceeding:	*25 – in science, research services, transportation, communications, services (with the exception of insurance companies); trade and public catering, and other non-manufacturing sectors.*
100 – in industry;	
30 – in agriculture and other manufacturing sectors;	
50 – in construction;	
20 – in retail trade, services, and other non-manufacturing sectors;	
30 – in wholesale trade and public catering.	

Source: Decree of the President of the Republic of Uzbekistan PP-1987 "On Amending the Decree 'On Measures to Promote the Further Development of Private Enterprises and Small Businesses'" from 9 April 1998, PP-3305', 30 August 2003.

ANNEX II

DEFINITION OF MEDIUM-SIZED, SMALL AND MICRO ENTERPRISES ACCORDING TO THE RECOMMENTATIONS OF THE EUROPEAN COMMISSION

ENTERPRISE CATEGORY	HEADCOUNT	TURNOVER	or	BALANCE SHEET TOTAL
MEDIUM-SIZED	<250	≤ € 50 million		≤ € 43 million
SMALL	<50	≤ € 10 million		≤ € 10 million
MICRO	<10	≤ € 2 million		≤ € 2 million

Source: Recommendation 2003/361/EC.

ANNEX III

CHANGES IN SIMPLIFIED ORDER OF TAXATION

15 April 1998

I. Single tax (until 1January 2003 was local tax; quarterly reporting) – for all MSEs

1 July 2003

I. Tax on gross revenues (monthly reporting):
a) all wholesale & retail sale enterprises (including MSEs);
b) all public catering enterprises (including MSEs)

II. Single tax (quarterly reporting) – for all MSEs

1 July 2005

I. Tax on gross revenues (quarterly reporting):
a) all wholesale & retail sale enterprises (including MSEs);
b) all public catering enterprises (including MSEs)

II. Single tax (quarterly reporting):
a) procurement and storage enterprises;
b) enterprises providing services under commission contracts;
c) brokerage enterprises

II. Single tax (quarterly reporting) – for the rest MSEs

III. Single tax payment (quarterly reporting) – for the rest MSEs

1 January 2007

I. Single tax payment (quarterly reporting) – for all MSEs

EFFECTS OF THE EXTENSION OF GEOGRAPHICAL INDICATIONS: A SOUTH ASIAN PERSPECTIVE

Surbhi Jain*

Geographical indications (GIs) associate names and places or production areas with products. They are distinctive signs that permit the identification of products on the market. GIs make it possible to add value to the natural riches of a country and to the skills of the population, and they give local products a distinguishable identity. If they are used in the proper way and are well protected, they can become an effective marketing tool of great economic value. The Agreement on Trade-Related Aspects of Intellectual Property Rights (TRIPS Agreement), which has more than 130 signatories, is the first international treaty to protect GIs through substantive provisions. In it, however, a clear distinction is made between the level of protection provided to wines and spirits and that provided to other products. Many countries, therefore, are actively working within the World Trade Organization to extend the existing protection that the Agreement grants to GIs for wines and spirits to GIs for all products. This paper is an attempt to analyse the issues relating to the scope extension of GIs under the TRIPS Agreement, especially with regard to South Asian countries. The paper argues that South Asian countries should equip their international property rights regimes to effectively protect the reputation of their geographical indications and their intrinsic qualities. In addition to the benefit of economies of scale, this would offer their products new opportunities in a competitive global market.

I. INTRODUCTION

The Agreement on Trade-Related Aspects of Intellectual Property Rights (TRIPS Agreement),[1] which came into force on 1 January 1995, is the most comprehensive multilateral agreement on intellectual property. It covers the main categories of intellectual property rights, establishes standards of protection as well as rules on enforcement, and

* Surbhi Jain is Deputy Director, Department of Commerce, Ministry of Commerce and Industry, New Delhi, India. The views expressed here are the author's alone and not those of the organization to which she belongs.

[1] The Agreement on Trade Related Aspects of Intellectual Property Rights (TRIPS Agreement) is an international agreement administered by the World Trade Organization that sets down minimum standards for many forms of intellectual property regulation. Specifically, the TRIPS Agreement contains requirements that nations' laws must meet with regard to: (a) copyright, including the rights of performers, producers of sound recordings and broadcasting organizations; (b) geographical indications, including appellations of origin; (c) industrial designs; (d) integrated circuit layout-designs; (e) patents; (f) monopolies for the developers of new plant varieties; (g) trademarks; (h) trade dress; and (i) undisclosed or confidential information. The legal text is available at www.wto.org/english/docs_e/legal_e/27-trips_01_e.htm.

provides for the application of the World Trade Organization (WTO)[2] dispute settlement mechanism for the resolution of disputes between WTO members. The intellectual property rights covered by the TRIPS Agreement are: copyrights and related rights; trademarks; geographical indications (GIs); industrial designs; patents; layout designs of integrated circuits; and protection of undisclosed information.

Geographical indications associate names and places or production areas with products. Scotch, Tequila, Bordeaux, Roquefort (cheese), Parma (ham) are prime examples of GIs as high-value commercial denominations. A whole section (Part II, section 3) of the TRIPS Agreement is dedicated to these geographical indications. GIs are distinctive signs which permit the identification of products on the market. If they are used in the proper way and are well protected, they can become an effective marketing tool of great economic value. GIs make it possible to add value to the natural riches of a country and to the skills of the population, and they give local products a distinguishable identity (Blakeney 2001).

The TRIPS Agreement, with more than 130 signatories, is the first international treaty which protects GIs through substantive provisions and provides an enforcement mechanism through WTO. In it, however, a clear distinction is made between the level of protection provided to wines and spirits and that provided to other products. Except for wines and spirits, it is all too easy to misuse GIs. Although a number of countries have developed effective legislation to protect GIs for all products, national regulations that apply only in one country are not sufficient in a global economy. Convinced of the economic benefit and great trade potential inherent in GIs, many countries around the world are actively working within WTO to have the existing protection granted by the Agreement to GIs for wines and spirits extended to cover GIs for all products (Escudero 2001).

The European Union seeks to use GI as a tool to consolidate the reputation and market niche of certain agricultural products, and to maintain its level of agricultural exports with regard to both quantity and value. The interests of the United States of America, on the other hand, relate to increased market access for agricultural products, and GI protection is seen as a potential protectionist barrier to such products. In general terms, the United States in its regional/bilateral agreements treats GIs as another form of trademark, thus emphasizing the exceptions clause under article 24.5 of the TRIPS Agreement. The European Union, in contrast, seeks to establish, through its regional/bilateral agreements, a sui generis form[3] of GI protection that clearly prevails over conflicting trademarks. Thus, the European Union seeks to eliminate the exceptions available under article 24.5 of the TRIPS Agreement. This has led to a stalemate at WTO regarding the scope extension of GIs (Das 2007).

---

[2] The World Trade Organization (WTO) provides a forum for negotiating agreements aimed at reducing obstacles to international trade and ensuring a level playing field for all, thus contributing to economic growth and development. WTO also provides a legal and institutional framework for the implementation and monitoring of these agreements, as well as for settling disputes arising from their interpretation and application. See www.wto.org/english/thewto_e/whatis_e/whatis_e.htm for details on the organization.

[3] Literally meaning "of its own kind".

This paper is an attempt to analyse the issues relating to the scope extension of GIs under the TRIPS Agreement. Section II will explain the conceptual differences between indications of source, appellations of origin and GIs. Section III focuses on the economic value of GIs. Section IV traces the historical background of TRIPS Agreement provisions on GIs. Section V discusses the inherent problems of the protection currently granted to GIs at the international level and the possible impact of the scope extension of GIs to products other than wines and spirits. Section VI discusses the implications of extended GIs for South Asia, with a special focus on India.

II. CONCEPTS

The terminology traditionally applied in treaties in the field of geographical indications administered by the World Intellectual Property Organization (WIPO)[4] distinguishes between "indications of source" and "appellations of origin" (WIPO 2001). The term "indication of source" is used in articles 1(2) and 10 of the Paris Convention for the Protection of Industrial Property (Paris Convention). It is also used throughout the Madrid Agreement for the Repression of False or Deceptive Indications of Source on Goods of 1891 (the Madrid Agreement). There is no definition of "indication of source" in those two treaties, but article 1(1) of the Madrid Agreement clarifies what is meant by the term: "All goods bearing a false or deceptive indication by which one of the countries to which this Agreement applies, or a place situated therein, is directly or indirectly indicated as being the country or place of origin shall be seized on importation into any of the said countries".

Consequently, an indication of source can be defined as an indication referring to a country, or to a place in that country, as being the country or place of origin of a product. It is important that the indication of source relates to the geographical origin of a product and not to another kind of origin, for example, an enterprise that manufactures the product. This definition does not imply any special quality or characteristics of the product on which an indication of source is used. Examples of indications of source are the mention, on a product, of the name of a country, or indications such as "made in ...".

The term "appellation of origin" is defined in the Lisbon Agreement for the Protection of Appellations of Origin and their International Registration of 1958 (Lisbon Agreement). The Agreement establishes an international system of protection for appellations of origin which are already protected under the national law of one of the State parties to that Agreement. Protection is subject to the international registration of that appellation of origin. Article 2(1) of the Lisbon Agreement defines the term "appellation of origin" as: "the geographical name of a country, region, or locality, which serves to designate a product originating therein, the quality and characteristics of which are due exclusively or essentially to the geographical environment, including natural and human factors".

Under this definition, an appellation of origin can be regarded as a special kind of indication of source, because the product for which an appellation of origin is used must have a quality and characteristics that are due exclusively or essentially to its origin. Examples of protected appellations of origin are Bordeaux (wine), Noix de Grenoble (nuts), tequila (spirit) and Jaffa (oranges).

The definition of geographical indication is given in part II, section 3, article 22.1 of the TRIPS Agreement: "Geographical indications are, for the purposes of this Agreement, indications which *identify a good* as originating in the territory of a Member [of WTO], or a region or locality in that territory, *where a given quality, reputation or other characteristic of the good is essentially attributable to its geographical origin*" (italics added).

According to this definition, a GI is an indication or sign borne by *any* product identified by the geographical indication as originating in a territory, region or locality, where (a) there is a specific quality, reputation or another characteristic inherent in these products, and (b) this quality, reputation or other characteristic is essentially attributable to the geographical origin of the products. This could, for example, include local geographical factors (such as climate and soil) or human factors present at the place of origin of the products (such as certain manufacturing techniques or a traditional production method).

The definition of a geographical indication is flexible enough, as it can protect the geographical names of localities, regions or countries or any name that evokes a geographical origin as long as the name meets the above requirements. At the same time, such a definition clearly excludes rules of origin or indications of source that indicate only the GI, but not any quality, reputation or other characteristic of the product. In this vein, rules of origin are a tool for tariff classification and must be distinguished from geographical indications within the meaning of the TRIPS Agreement (Addor and Grazioli 2002).

If the definitions of indication of source, appellation of origin and geographical indication are compared, the following can be observed. Indication of source is the broadest term; it comprises both geographical indication and appellation of origin. Indications of source require only that the product on which the indication of source is used originate in a certain geographical area (made in ...). Thus, there are indications of source that would seem not to be covered by the definition of geographical indication under the TRIPS Agreement, namely those whose use on products does not imply a particular quality, reputation or characteristic of those products. Geographical indications are more broadly defined than appellations of origin. In other words, all appellations of origin are geographical indications, but some geographical indications are not appellations of origin.

III. ECONOMIC AND SOCIAL RATIONALE OF GEOGRAPHICAL INDICATIONS

The basic economic function of geographical indications is to protect the goodwill of products to which they relate. There is no agreed definition of goodwill, at least in international trademark law. It can be conveniently defined as the "tendency or likelihood of a consumer to repurchase goods or services based upon the name or source of goods and services" (WIPO 2003).

Although goodwill is not the same as, say, an invention or a copyrighted work, it is equally intangible and thus possesses the same public-good property—it may be used on any number of related goods or services. Therefore, an unauthorized exploitation of a trademark's goodwill is, from an economic point of view, always feasible (Rangnekar 2002). It is no wonder then that the unauthorized use of a trademark has been recognized as a legal issue for quite some time and is known in law as counterfeiting. The TRIPS Agreement defines counterfeiting, in a footnote to article 51 in section 4, as follows: "counterfeit trademark goods shall mean any goods, including packaging, bearing without authorization a trademark which is identical to the trademark validly registered in respect of such goods, or which cannot be distinguished in its essential aspects from such trademark, and which thereby infringes the rights of the owner of the trademark in question under the law of the country of importation".

There is, however, an additional economic impact of geographical indications. By virtue of their basic function of distinguishing the goods or services of one enterprise from the same or similar goods or services of other enterprises, trademarks are the main building block of market identity (Das 2007). The notion of market identity can be best explained by a simple analogy. It can be said that trademarks play the same role in the identification of goods or services as personal names play in the identification of individuals. Similar reasoning applies to geographical indications, although they relate to a group of enterprises rather than a single enterprise. It can also be said that geographical indications play the same role as citizenship. Market identity significantly encourages inventive and other creative activity. After all, a product based on a highly valuable invention can succeed on the market only if the product itself is recognized to be innovative—but this recognition can be achieved only with the assistance of branding, that is, with trademarks and/or geographical indications. In other words, success based on inventive activity depends on the success of market identity, whereas the reverse does not necessarily hold true.

GIs serve to protect intangible assets such as market differentiation, reputation and quality standards. They enable the linking of a specific product to the territory from which it originates. GIs convey the cultural identity of a nation, region or a locality and add a human dimension to goods that are increasingly subject to standardized production for mass consumption. GIs are understood by customers to denote the origin and the quality of products. GIs are increasingly recognized as a tool for securing consumers' loyalty by establishing the link between product attributes and the geographical origin. In economic terms, a GI essentially enables producers to increase profits through product differentiation (Chaturvedi 2002).

Many GIs have acquired valuable reputations which, if not adequately protected, could be misrepresented by dishonest commercial operators. False use of GIs by unauthorized parties is detrimental to consumers and legitimate producers. The former are deceived and are falsely led into believing that they are buying a genuine product with specific qualities and characteristics while they in fact get an imitation. The latter suffer damage because valuable business is taken away from them and the established reputation for their products is damaged.

GIs as an instrument of intellectual property protection have specific features that, in contrast to other intellectual property rights (IPRs), are considered relatively more amenable to the customary practices of indigenous communities (UNDP 2007). As no institution (firm or individual) exercises exclusive monopoly control over the knowledge or information embedded in the protected indication (or the good), it remains in the public domain. Many indigenous communities consider their knowledge as a heritage to be protected for the lifetime of their culture. A particular indication is protected as long as the good-place-quality link is maintained and the indication not rendered generic.

Traditional knowledge and GIs share a common element insofar as they both protect accumulated knowledge typical to a specific locality. While traditional knowledge expresses the local traditions of knowledge, GIs stand for the specific geographical origin of a typical product or production method. Traditional knowledge establishes a social relationship between the product and a person, while GIs are traditional insofar as they represent food and production systems endogenous to a specific region. Geographical indications may substitute for intellectual property protection of traditional knowledge (Panizzon 2006). As such, fears of the commodification of traditional knowledge on account of GIs are not entirely valid. To the extent that products draw on distinctive traditional methods of production that have been preserved and nurtured over time by communities specific to a region, GIs can be used as a legal tool to develop, market and protect a brand.

A GI is a collective right that is open to all producers in the region that observe the specified codes and produce in the demarcated geographical region. The "holders" of a GI do not have the right to assign the indication, which is provided to holders of trademarks (article 20 of the TRIPS Agreement) and patents (article 28.2, TRIPS Agreement). Closely following this, the good-place link underlying GI protection automatically prohibits the transfer of the indication to producers outside the demarcated region. Nor can the indication be used on similar goods originating from outside the designated geographical area. In effect, the result of protection is to limit the class and/or location of people who may use the protected indication. GI protection, however, is no guarantee against the misappropriation of traditional knowledge, and other strategies to protect such knowledge must be adopted. Yet GIs remain meaningful in enabling "people to translate their long-standing, collective, and patrimonial knowledge into livelihood and income" (Bérard and Marchenay 1996).

IV. HISTORICAL BACKGROUND OF THE PROVISIONS OF THE TRIPS AGREEMENT

Prior to the TRIPS Agreement, some international treaties, such as the Paris Convention, the Madrid Agreement and the Lisbon Agreement, contained provisions on the protection of indication of source and appellations of origin. Even though some of these treaties contained strong provisions for the protection of appellations of origin, their practical results were meagre. First, because the Paris Convention included only a general provision on this matter, and second, because the Madrid and Lisbon Agreements had limited membership.

The Paris Convention

The Paris Convention was agreed in 1883 and complemented by the Madrid Protocol of 1891. It was revised at Brussels (1900), Washington D.C. (1911), The Hague (1925), London (1934), Lisbon (1958) and Stockholm (1967), and amended in 1979. The Paris Convention, as of 22 October 2009, had 173 signatory states.

This treaty was the first multilateral agreement to provide protection for indications of source and appellations of origin. Article 1(2) of the Paris Convention includes indications of source and appellations of origin as aspects of industrial property protection. Article 10(1) provides for indications of source the same remedies prescribed in respect of goods unlawfully bearing a trademark or a trade name "in cases of direct or indirect use of a false indication of source of the goods or the identity of the producer, manufacturer, or merchant".

According to the Convention, the main remedies for unlawfully bearing an indication of source are seizure of the product upon importation, or at least prohibition of importation, or seizure within the country. Article 10*bis* of the Paris Convention obliges members to provide protection against unfair competition and contains a non-exhaustive list of some acts that are to be prohibited. This provision gives the basis for the protection against misleading indications of source, including appellations of origin. The Paris Convention does not provide for any remedies in case of infringement of this provision.

The Madrid Agreement

The Madrid Agreement was adopted in 1891 and revised at Washington D.C. (1911), The Hague (1925), London (1934), and Lisbon (1958). It was supplemented by the Additional Act of Stockholm (1967), and had a membership of 35 signatory states as of 22 October 2009. In the last 25 years (1985-2009), only six new States have become parties to the treaty. Unlike the Paris Convention, which is a general treaty that provides protection for a broad range of different categories of industrial property rights, the Madrid Agreement provides specific rules for the repression of false and deceptive indications of source.

The Agreement establishes rules on how seizure should take place and defines the competent authority to enforce these kinds of measures. It also contains a special provision by which the courts of each country can decide what indications of source do not fall within the provisions of the Agreement, because of their generic character; regional appellations concerning the source of products of the vine are excluded from such a reservation. This provision, in article 4 of the Agreement, could be considered the reasons why sectoral geographical indications need special protection, especially those concerning wines and spirits. Finally, it should be noted that GIs can be protected as collective marks, certification marks or guarantee marks.

The Lisbon Agreement

This Agreement was concluded in Lisbon on 31 October 1958. It was revised in Stockholm in 1967 and amended in 1979. Any member of the Paris Convention may accede to the treaty. As of 19 October 2009, there were 26 States party to the Agreement. In the last 20 years (1989-2009) only 10 new States have acceded to the Agreement. There are two basic requirements for an appellation of origin to be protected, in accordance with the terms of this Agreement: (a) the appellation of origin should be protected in its country of origin; and (b) the appellation of origin should be registered in the International Register of WIPO.

According to the Regulations under the Lisbon Agreement for the Protection of Appellations of Origin and their International Registration, applications for the international registration of an appellation of origin are to be addressed to the International Bureau in Geneva by the competent office of the country of whose name, or the country in which is situated the region or locality whose name constitutes the appellation of origin which has given the product its reputation.

TRIPS Agreement

Another of the important features of the TRIPS Agreement, with regard to geographical indications, is that it is bound to enforce its application according to minimum standards. It also provides a strong dispute settlement mechanism under the WTO system. Article 71 of the TRIPS Agreement provides for periodic review and article 23 provides for negotiations aimed at increasing the protection of individual geographical indications. As stated, the TRIPS Agreement is the first international treaty providing wide coverage for geographical indications, and has the largest signatory membership on this issue. The provisions contained in section 3 of the Agreement were the result of a complex and difficult process of negotiations.

The Agreement contains a clear triple distinction in the level of protection for geographical indications related to (a) all products, (b) wines and spirits, and (c) wines only. The Agreement, at the time of its adoption, represented the particular interest of the European wine-producing countries, which supported stronger and special protection to this kind of product, compared to the standard protection granted to other products.

Since the adoption of the TRIPS Agreement, signatory countries have become more aware of the need for sufficient protection of geographical indications for all products. Also, the ongoing negotiations in the field of industrial and agricultural products, as pursued by WTO, reflects the growing importance of extending the level of protection given to geographical indications for wines and spirits to all products. Such protection is an invaluable marketing tool and an added value for exports, because it increases the chances of market access for such goods. The extension of the additional protection of article 23 to geographical indications for products other than wines and spirits must be part of the global vision of a multilateral trade system (WTO 2008).

V. ADDITIONAL LEVEL OF PROTECTION TO WINES AND SPIRITS: SOME ISSUES

Article 22.1 of the TRIPS Agreement defines geographical indications which are protected by the TRIPS Agreement (see section II). While there is just one definition for all geographical indications, part II, section 3 of the TRIPS Agreement provides for two different levels of protection.

Article 22 covers geographical indications for products other than wines and spirits. In contrast to article 23, article 22 limits the protection of geographical indications to cases where the public is misled by the use of a geographical indication as to the true geographical origin of the product, or where such use constitutes an act of unfair competition (the "misleading test").

Article 23 provides for additional protection of geographical indications in the category of wines and spirits. Under Article 23, there is no need to prove that the public is misled or that using a certain geographical indication constitutes unfair competition. The use of accompanying expressions such as "style", "type", "kind" and "imitation" are prohibited and protection is also provided when the indication is used in translated form. The burden of proof does not rest with the plaintiff (WIPO 2001). Under article 23, competitors not producing within the geographical area are simply prevented from using the corresponding denomination, and they may not use trademarks containing or consisting of geographical indications used to identify wines or spirits (subject to the exceptions provided for in article 24).

Exceptions under article 23.1

A term claimed as a GI must fit the criteria set out in the TRIPS definition mentioned above. Even if the product meets this definition, several important exceptions can render some terms non-protectable, at least in the territories of some members:

(a) Some existing use would be preserved. Article 24.4 grandfathers[5] the existing use of GIs for wine and spirits, and this could be extended to all products if article 23.1 was extended. This means that it might not be possible to prevent other members from using a GI that they are already using domestically;

(b) Generic[6] terms would remain non-protectable. A term that has already become generic in a particular country would remain generic and non-protectable, despite

---

[5] The World Intellectual Property Organization (WIPO) was established by the WIPO Convention in 1967 with a mandate from its Member States to promote the protection of intellectual property throughout the world through cooperation among states and in collaboration with other international organizations. For more information, see www.wipo.int/portal/index.html.en.

[6] This is true if such symbols are capable of indicating the origin of the goods without literally naming the place of their origin, for example, basmati.

the extension of coverage (article 24.6). This exception could affect terms with geographical origins that have become well known globally (for example Cheddar cheese);

(c) Failure to protect in the country of origin removes others' obligation to protect. Before a member could expect to obtain protection of its GIs in the countries of other members, it would have to provide *domestic* protection for those GIs (article 24.9). That protection might have to be at the article 23 level. For the reasons set out below, this could place onerous obligations on all members.

Aside from these exceptions, the protection article 23 affords geographical indications for wines and spirits is notably enhanced compared to that provided in article 22 for other products, which relies on the "misleading test". The limited protection granted by article 22 has several deficiencies.

Free riding

In order for the protection of Article 22 of the TRIPS Agreement to apply, the undue use of a geographical indication has to mislead the public as to the geographical origin of the product or must constitute an act of unfair competition. The same applies to refusing or invalidating the registration of a trademark containing or consisting of a geographical indication with respect to goods not originating in the territory indicated.

The requirement of the "misleading test" in article 22 is tailored to suit unfair competition or consumer protection regulations. Compared to the protection granted by article 23 to geographical indications for wines and spirits, however, it does not provide sufficient intellectual property protection for the benefit of the producers entitled to use a geographical indication. It enables free riding by other producers on the renown of a geographical indication. A producer may use a geographical indication for his product, even if it does not originate in the territory purported, as long as the product's true origin is indicated on the label. Thus, a producer can profit from the use of a famous geographical indication and argue that it is not misleading the consumer. One example of such misguidance is a case where a producer uses the geographical indication Geneva on a clock-face even though the clock does not originate from Geneva, but engraves the true origin on the back of the clock.

Legal uncertainty

The requirement of the "misleading test" results in legal uncertainty as to the enforcement of protection for an individual geographical indication at the international level. It is up to the national courts and the national administrative authorities to decide whether or not the public is being misled by a particular use of a geographical indication, and to enforce their decision. However, whether or not the public is being misled and how the legal and administrative authorities apply and interpret this discretionary element of "misleading the public" differs from country to country, resulting in inconsistent decisions. Such legal uncertainty undermines and damages the good functioning of international trade in goods having the added value of a geographical indication. It can be avoided by granting the level of protection as provided by article 23 of the TRIPS Agreement, which does not require the "misleading test" or evidence of unfair competition, to all geographical indications.

Burden of proof

The "misleading test" carries another disadvantage, namely, in order to defend a geographical indication for a product under this article, it is up to the plaintiff to prove to judicial or administrative authorities that the public has been misled, or that there has been an act of unfair competition. This is complicated and expensive. There is no such burden of proof put on the producer in the domain of geographical indications for wines and spirits. In contrast, article 23 specifically prohibits per se the use of geographical indications for wines and spirits not originating in the place indicated by the geographical indication. This standard of protection should apply to geographical indications for other products as well.

Extending the scope of article 23.1 of the TRIPS Agreement

The practical effect of article 23.1 is to permit interested parties to prevent, without having to prove that the public is misled or that there is an act of unfair competition:

(a) The use of the geographical indication by others, generally, for products not originating in the place indicated by the geographical indication in question (e.g., unqualified use of Napa Valley by French producers in France);

(b) The use of the geographical indication even in conjunction with an additional indication in which the true place of origin of the products is indicated (for example, Napa Valley of France);

(c) The use of the geographical indication even if the geographical indication is used in translation (for example, Valle de los Cactus);

(d) The use of the geographical indication if is accompanied by expression such as "kind", "type", "style" or "imitation" (for example, Napa Valley type).

This protection is supplemented by that of article 22.2(b), which seeks to prevent other illegitimate uses of the terms or signs that are not contemplated specifically by article 23.1, also covering cases where a geographical indication denoting a special kind of product is used in the designation or presentation of another category of products.

The extension of article 23.1 of the TRIPS Agreement to products other than wines and spirits has no implications for the definition of article 22.1, as this debate concerns only the different level of protection between geographical indications for wines and spirits and those for other products. However, it is important to note that the TRIPS definition of geographical indications does not distinguish between products and, therefore, constitutes both a premise and a precedent of harmonious, balanced protection of all geographical indications on all products.

The anomaly of inconsistent treatment

Geographical indications stand on an equal footing with other intellectual property rights such as trademarks or copyright. In none of the other fields of intellectual property rights is a difference made in the level of protection of those rights according to product categories. A uniform level of protection applies. There are no logical or legal reasons that could justify two different levels of protection in the field of geographical indications.

It is the absence of article 23 cover for these other GIs that enables competitors from outside a region to usurp the reputation of a GI, thereby dividing a considerable share of the market away from the legitimate right holders. This kind of illegitimate practice not only damages the reputation of the original GI, but also deprives the genuine right holders of the full benefit of the investments they put into developing their goods and creating goodwill and reputation in the market. Consumers are also likely to be misled into thinking that they are purchasing an authentic good with a certain well-specified quality and characteristics, whereas they are actually buying an imitation (WTO 2001a).

No substantive justification for discriminatory treatment

To treat geographical indications for wines and spirits differently from those for other products is substantively unjustified. The geographical origin confers, whether due to natural or human factors, intrinsic qualities to a good that a similar product without this origin will not have. The geographical origin, from a commercial point of view, has the same importance for all products. Often, the trade value of geographical indications for products other than wines and spirits is even higher than a specific geographical indication for a wine or a spirit. Examples include famous geographical indications such as Darjeeling tea, Carolina rice, Maine lobster and Bukhara carpets. With the extension of article 23, the existing imbalance of section 3 will disappear, providing the same level of effective protection to geographical indications for all products.

The rationale behind extension

A solid case can be made for extending protection, as outlined below:

(a) The TRIPS Agreement would ensure the same protection for all geographical indications, irrespective of the product. The protection currently provided for geographical indications for products other than wines and spirits is inadequate. It does not prevent products whose names are ineligible for the geographical indication from free riding on the reputation of genuine geographical indications;

this harms legitimate producers and the marketing of products actually originating from the place indicated by the geographical indication. Extension would provide an adequate level of protection to geographical indications for all products (WTO 2001b);

(b) Currently there are no economic or systemic reasons why certain types of products should have more protection for geographical indications. The risk of confusion between products originating in a specific region and having a special quality due to that origin, on the one hand, and products using the same denomination but not having the qualities derived from that specific region, on the other, is important and damaging for any product, not just for wines and spirits;

(c) Legitimate producers of a product identified by a geographical indication would be better protected against illegal use of the GI of such category of products. Competitors not producing such product within the indicated geographical area would be prevented from illegitimately using the geographical indication of such products. Hence all producers would have a clear view of the situations in which use of a GI for products of the same category is lawful or not. Legitimate users of GIs would not have to undergo costly procedures to demonstrate that the consumer is confused as the applicable test of article 23.1 of the TRIPS Agreement (that is, whether the geographical indication is used on a product not originating in the place referred by the geographical indication) is easier to ascertain than the one required by article 22.2. The test would therefore be made objective and judicial decisions would be uniform and harmonious, as the final decision is not left to the judge's perception of whether the public is actually misled (WTO 2002);

(d) Illegitimate use of a geographical indication with a *délocalisant* (that is, semi-generics) indicating the true origin or use in translation or with expression such as "kind", "type", "style" or "imitation" would be prevented for all geographical indications and would help prevent more GIs from becoming generic and gradually losing all economic value;

(e) Extended protection of GIs facilitates product identification by the consumer. Consumer choice is enhanced;

(f) Extension would open new market opportunities by preventing trade distortions. The benefits would foster the development of local rural communities and encourage a quality agricultural and industrial policy. As is the case for products protected via trademarks, those covered by adequate GI protection would be in a better position to benefit from enhanced access to third-country markets. As such, a GI regime would bring economic benefits to producers worldwide, not only to producers in countries where the local protection of GIs is already stronger than in WTO;

(g) The creation of comprehensive GI protection is not incompatible with the smooth future development of business activities that take place in one WTO member State on the basis of denominations protected in other WTO member States on an exclusive basis. The same problem has been satisfactorily addressed in the context of wines and spirits as the TRIPS Agreement already provides enough elements of flexibility, such as exceptions and transitional periods, to ensure that trade flows are not disrupted. Transitional periods and exceptions can accommodate the interests of producers and make re-labelling unnecessary. Therefore, extension as such would not affect the production and exportation of products;

(h) Introducing a domestic GI legislation and implementing any new law entails administrative costs. Because the TRIPS Agreement leaves the actual implementation decision to WTO members, it is not clear how much a higher level of protection for other products would actually cost. Extending the level of protection to other products does not in and of itself entail new costs, but would impose new costs to those countries that want to claim GIs on other products for the first time. However, extending the type of protection afforded to wine and spirits under the TRIPS Agreement could lower the legal costs of enforcing GIs by making enforcement decisions less subjective.

The relationship between trademarks and GIs

Geographical indications and trademarks are two distinct categories of intellectual property rights that might enter into conflict. The TRIPS Agreement devotes articles 23.2 and 22.3 to those conflicts when they concern wines and spirits or other products, respectively.

Article 23.2 of the TRIPS Agreement establishes that "the registration of a trademark for wines which contains or consists of a geographical indication identifying wines or for spirits which contains or consists of a geographical indication identifying spirits shall be refused or invalidated, ex officio if a Member's legislation so permits or at the request of an interested party, with respect to such wines or spirits not having this origin".

Article 22.3 sets out a different rule for GIs for non-wines and spirits by establishing that "a Member shall, ex officio if its legislation so permits or at the request of an interested party, refuse or invalidate the registration of a trademark which contains or consists of a geographical indication with respect to goods not originating in the territory indicated, if use of the indication in the trademark for such goods in that Member is of such a nature as to mislead the public as to the true place of origin". This article does not come into play in the case of the registration of a trademark which contains or consists of a GI identifying another category of products as the one identified by the GI. In such circumstances, the general standard protection of article 22.3 applies.

To sum up, the protection currently granted by articles 22.3 and 23.2 of the TRIPS Agreement precludes the registration and validity of registered trademarks containing or consisting of geographical indications when they are borne by wines and spirits and permitted when they are borne by other products, if they do not mislead the public.

As extension would make article 23.2 applicable to all products, the reference in article 23.2 to wines and spirits would be no longer necessary and should be replaced by a reference to "products of the same category not having that origin". This would facilitate the examination of the trademarks by administrative authorities, trademark registrars or judges. Such reviewers would refer to a simple, objective criterion (that is, do the products identified by a trademark, which contains or consists of a GI, really have the geographical origin referred by the GI?) when deciding whether or not to refuse the registration of a trademark, if their legislation so permits, or to invalidate the trademark for products not originating in the indicated region. In addition, the legitimate producers and other interested parties (for example, legitimate producers from the geographical location, representative associations from those areas, or even consumer associations) would obtain a more effective and less costly protection of their GIs against trademarks. Trademark holders and applicants would also have a clearer vision of whether a trademark containing a geographical indication could be used or not. This would also be instrumental in clarifying the relationship between trademarks and geographical indications.

Establishment of a multilateral system of notification and registration of GIs

Article 23.4 of the TRIPS Agreement provides for the establishment of a multilateral system of notification and registration of GIs for wines. The Singapore Ministerial Declaration of 1996 extended the provision to spirits as well. If extended, such a system would contribute to the implementation of more effective GI protection in genera . A coherent approach would suggest that the systems be open to all GIs. This would facilitate the burden of proof of the plaintiffs and the workload of the judges when having to decide on the legitimacy of the use of a GI. Such a register would serve as a helpful reference to civil and administrative authorities.

Therefore, it seems necessary that nothing in article 23.4 should prevent a system of notification and registration of geographical indications from being open to any GI that meets the definition of article 22.1 of the TRIPS Agreement. This issue, however, is being discussed separately from the question of extension at the WTO forum.

VI. APPLICATION IN SOUTH ASIA

The case of basmati rice is well known. Basmati, a variety of *Oryza sativa*, is the fragrant, long, slender rice with a nutty flavour that has been grown in the northern parts of the Indian subcontinent for hundreds of years. Among the hundred or more types of aromatic rice in the world, basmati is probably the most expensive—India earns over $400 million annually in basmati exports. In September 1997, Texas-based RiceTec Inc. was awarded Patent No. 5663484 on basmati rice lines and grains by the United States Patent and Trademark Office (USPTO). This caused a furore in the subcontinent, and provoked India to lodge an immediate protest. RiceTec had made 20 patent claims, essentially covering: (a) rice plants with characteristics identical to basmati; (b) grain produced by such plants; and (c) a method of selecting rice plants, based on the starch index test. Following the challenge by India, in September 2000 RiceTec withdrew 4 of its 20 claims. In March 2001, USPTO told RiceTec that, of its remaining claims, only three were approved, issuing it a varietal patent to market the types of basmati developed by it, and not cultivated and bred traditionally by farmers in India and Pakistan. Together, India and Pakistan need to fight for a GI for basmati to protect their export markets.

Other well-known examples of GIs in South Asia include: Himalayan waters, Alphonso and Sindhri mangoes, Bhutanese red rice, Pakistani shu (windproof woollen fabric) and ajrak (designs from Sindh), jasmine (Hom Mali) rice, Ceylon and Darjeeling teas, and Phulkari of Pakistan, among others. India, Pakistan and Sri Lanka have taken a stand internationally in favour of extending GI protection to products other than wines and spirits.

Development implications of GIs

Explicit economic gains are important, but issues of community rights to ownership of traditional knowledge, consumer welfare and global equity are development goals worth pursuing for their own intrinsic merits. GIs have an important bearing on the four dimensions of human development: empowerment, productivity, equity and sustainability. They confer on owners legitimate rights, empowering them; they offer opportunities to make productive use of those rights which, given the characteristics of the assumed owners of these rights (mostly low-income agricultural and artisanal societies), can be expected to contribute to an equitable distribution of benefits. The legal-economic incentives could then create a virtuous cycle of other incentives to nurture and sustain traditional methods and know-how, which could contribute to intergenerational equity.

South Asian countries should take this up as a development issue, as geographical indications are linked with the livelihoods of the people residing the designated areas. Most GIs in South Asia are linked to products related to agriculture, fisheries, crafts and artisanal works, which are also some of the sectors that provide livelihoods to large sections of the poor. In order to examine the socio-economic implications of a GI, the entire supply chain of the product concerned needs to be examined. While GI protection may indeed strengthen the sector concerned by yielding financial benefits, these benefits may not be shared equitably among various stakeholders along the supply chain of the product. If the higher price commanded by the product on account of GI protection is confined to the more powerful actors on the upper stream of the supply chain and do not filter down to the weaker sections of the chain, it will nullify the development implications of GI protection. Given such possibilities, the realities on the ground of the impact of GI protection on rural development in the region are worth investigating.

For a start, countries in South Asia need to provide IPR protection at home first, as domestic protection is an essential prerequisite for TRIPS Agreement protection. GI registration, in itself, builds up valuable reputations and goodwill. Creating a national catalogue of GIs marries the old and the new: the national imperative of creating awareness about traditional products and knowledge, with preparedness to engage internationally with the trade of goods and ideas in the twenty-first century (UNDP 2007). Thus, countries in the subregion will need to strengthen their databases on GIs, their socio-economic and cultural values, associated features such as the microenterprises they can spin off, and their attraction for tourism or investment. Anticipating more sophisticated cases of disputes over GIs, there is a need to determine and codify scientific attributes of their products on which legal verdicts can be based, instead of relying on subjective, connoisseur-determined statements on reputation, as is largely the case now (Das 2007).

IPR regimes of the South Asian countries[7]

IPR regimes in Pakistan, Sri Lanka and India are in their infancy, while Afghanistan, Nepal and Bhutan are very small players in world trade.

Pakistan

Pakistan does not have a sui generis system of GI protection yet. GIs receive some protection under the country's Trade Marks Ordinance, 2001 and Trade Marks Rules, 2004. This includes:

(a) Special laws for the protection of geographical indications or appellations of origin;

(b) Trademark laws in the form of collective marks or certification marks;

(c) Laws against unfair competition;

(d) Consumer protection laws;

(e) Specific laws or decrees that recognize individual geographical indications.

A draft Ordinance on GIs of Goods (Registration and Protection) has not yet been promulgated due to expert criticism that it is vague. Pakistan, nonetheless, foresees a registration system akin to that of trademarks, whereby community applicants file an application, which is then examined by a Registrar of GIs for its merit; factors such as prior registration and public opposition would also be addressed. Work on GIs in Pakistan is new; awareness grew after the above-mentioned patenting of basmati grains and lines.

Sri Lanka

Sri Lanka relies overwhelmingly on its most famous GI, Ceylon tea, which brings in nearly $700 million in annual export earnings and provides employment to over 1 million people. The country has drawn up its own provisions for protecting GIs: part IX, chapter

---

[7] Information for this section has been gathered from the respective websites of Government authorities related to the protection of intellectual property.

XXXIII under the new Intellectual Property Act, passed on 12 November 2003. Its definition and scope of protection go beyond the TRIPS Agreement by extending stronger protection to agricultural products on par with wines and spirits. The Act's definition of GI is identical to article 22.1 of the TRIPS Agreement, and it also has a provision for homonymous GIs.

Although it has a sui generis system of GI protection, Sri Lanka has not opted for a registration system. Some critics note that this type of GI protection is akin to copyright protection, and hence vulnerable. GI protection is also offered through trademark laws; however, these place most of the burden on the country's courts and the industries, which are required to seek remedies in the form of injunctions or damages.

The new laws on GIs in Sri Lanka do not cover handicrafts and fishery products, and they could be said to be less comprehensive than their Indian counterparts. In addition to the separate section on GIs, the Intellectual Property Act also accords protection through section 103 (marks), sections 160 and 161 (unfair competition) and under offences and penalties for a false declaration of a GI.

India

The definition of GIs included in section 1(3)(e) of the Geographical Indication of Goods (Registration and Protection) Act 1999 is as follows:

"[G]eographical indication", in relation to goods, means an indication which identifies such goods as agricultural goods, natural goods or manufactured goods as originating, or manufactured in the territory of a country, or a region or locality in that territory, where a given quality, reputation or other characteristic of such goods is essentially attributable to its geographical origin and in case where such goods are manufactured goods one of the activities of either the production or of processing or preparation of the goods concerned takes place in such territory, region or locality, as the case may be.

The explanation added to this definition adds: "for the purposes of this clause, any name which is not the name of a country, region or locality of that country shall also be considered as the geographical indication if it relates to a specific geographical area and is used upon or in relation to particular goods origination from that country, region or locality, as the case may be". This clearly leaves room for providing protection to symbols[8] as well as geographical names. Notably, while the TRIPS Agreement (article 22.1) requires "a given quality, reputation or other characteristic" of the good to be essentially attributable to its geographical origin, the Geographical Indication of Goods (Registration and Protection) Act, in the case of manufactured goods, includes the additional requirement that one of the activities of either the production, processing or preparation of the good concerned must be carried out in the place of its geographical origin. This requirement is more stringent than that under article 22.1 of the TRIPS Agreement.

---

[8] This is true if such symbols are capable of indicating the origin of the goods without literally naming the place of their origin, for example, basmati.

Section 11(2)(a) of the Act stipulates what an application for registration should contain and refers to the "geographical environment, with its inherent natural and human factors". Notably, the inclusion of human factors becomes vital for India, to ensure that potential GIs associated with various handicraft products of Indian origin also get protected. For instance, Kancheepuram silk is a product of skilled labour from Tamil Nadu; Kolhapuri chappals are products of skilled labour from Maharashtra. The TRIPS Agreement is silent on whether the requirements implied may be attributed to natural factors (for example, climate), or whether those characteristics that result from human factors (such as artisans residing in a particular region) may also be covered under the definition contained in article 22.1.

The counterpart of article 22.2 of the TRIPS Agreement can be found in section 21(1)(a) of the Geographical Indication of Goods (Registration and Protection) Act, which gives the proprietor and authorized users of a registered GI the right to prevent any infringement of the GI concerned. The provision related to trademarks under article 22.3 of the TRIPS Agreement has been complied with in section 25(a) of the Act. Article 23.1 of the TRIPS Agreement relates to wines and spirits alone, while under the Act, the central Government has been given the discretion to accord additional protection to goods notified in the official Gazette.

A Geographical Indications Registry with all-India jurisdiction operates in Chennai, as per the Act. Agricultural, natural or manufactured goods can be registered as GIs if they fall under the definition in section 1(3)(e) of the Act, as described above. Ultimately, eligibility is determined by the Registrar of Geographical Indications, on receipt of the application.

GI registration gives to the registered proprietor and its authorized users the legal right to the exclusive use of the GI and also the right to obtain relief in case of its infringement. The exclusion of unauthorized persons from misusing GI would ensure that genuine products of the rightful producers are marketed. The registration of a GI is valid for 10 years and can be renewed successively for further periods of 10 years. A registered GI cannot be assigned, transmitted, mortgaged, pledged or licensed. Under the Geographical Indications of Goods (Registration & Protection) Act, any association of persons, producers, organization or authority established by or under the law can apply for protection of a GI. The only criterion is that the applicant must represent the interest of the producers.

VII. CONCLUSION

Effective protection involves a balance of interests between consumers, producers and governments. Consumers have an interest in not being misled by geographical indications, producers have a trade interest in protecting those reputational characteristics of a product that are related to its geographical origin, and governments have an interest in ensuring that international obligations relating to geographical indications are administered in an efficient and equitable manner. Opponents of extended protection for all GIs argue that such conditions would effectively be protectionism. In their view, GIs are a means to close off future market access opportunities for emerging industries. However, GIs have no exclusive character with regard to production. Anyone outside the designated area can still produce and sell the goods in question, just under another name. The benefits of extending GI protection can be summed up as follows:

(a) The cost of extension, if any, would be more than offset by the benefits of more effective protection of geographical indications in world trade;

(b) Extension does not require the establishment of a new legal or administrative protection regime such as a register, but merely an extension to other products of the protection members already must provide wines and spirits under article 23 of the TRIPS Agreement;

(c) Extension facilitates the protection and enforcement of geographical indications, since the "misleading test" and/or the proof of a case of unfair competition would no longer have to be established. Extension therefore could represent a cost savings for judicial and administrative authorities as well as for those who are entitled to the use of a geographical indication and interested in the enforcement of their right against misuse;

(d) The purpose of extension is not to benefit those members with a large number of geographical indications at the expense of those with few. The aim is to achieve a level playing field in the TRIPS Agreement for all geographical indications, enabling all members and their products to benefit from the additional, more effective protection;

(e) Extension would prevent further geographical indications from becoming generic through the misuse of such indications in translations or through delocalization. Considering the exceptions from protection as contained in article 24 of the TRIPS Agreement, extension is of particular interest and benefit to those members who make use of their GIs and intend to develop them as a marketing tool for their products.

In conclusion, extending the protection of GIs for wines and spirits to include GIs for other products would benefit all members. South Asian countries should equip their IPR regimes to effectively protect the reputation of their GIs and their intrinsic qualities. In addition to the benefit of economies of scale, this could offer their products new opportunities in a competitive global market. The freer trade is, the more important the protection of geographical indications becomes.

REFERENCES

Addor, F. and A. Grazioli (2002). "GIs beyond wines and spirits—a roadmap for better protection for GIs", *Journal of World Intellectual Property*, vol. 5, No. 6, November, pp. 863-97.

Bérard and Marchenay (1996), "Tradition, regulation and intellectual property: local agricultural products and foodstuffs in France", in S.B. Brush and D. Stabinsky, eds., *Valuing Local Knowledge: Indigenous Peoples and Intellectual Property Rights*, as cited in D. Rangnekar (2003), "The socio-economics of geographical indications: a review of empirical evidence from Europe", Issue Paper No. 8, UNCTAD/ICTSD Capacity Building Project on Intellectual Property Rights and Sustainable Development.

Blakeney, M. (2001). "Geographical indications and TRIPS", Occasional paper No. 8 (Geneva, Quaker United Nations Office).

Chaturvedi, S. (2002). "India, EU & GI: convergence of interest and challenges ahead", RIS discussion paper, No. 35/2002.

Das, K. (2007). "Protection of geographical indications: an overview of select issues with particular reference to India", CENTAD Working Paper 8.

Escudero, S. (2001). "International protection of geographical indications and developing countries", T.R.A.D.E. Working Paper 10 (Geneva, South Centre).

Panizzon, M. (2006). "Traditional knowledge and geographical indications: foundations, interests and negotiating positions", NCCR Trade Working Paper No. 2005/01.

Rangnekar, D. (2002). "Geographical indications: a review of proposals at the TRIPs council: extending Article 23 to products other than wines and spirits", Issue Paper No. 4, UNCTAD/ICTSD Capacity Building Project on Intellectual Property Rights and Sustainable Development.

United Nations Development Programme (UNDP) (2007). "Geographical indications as trade-related intellectual property", UNDP discussion paper, accessed from www.undprcc.lk/Publications/Publications/TRADE/GI_Paper_13_Dec.pdf.

World Intellectual Property Organization–International Bureau (WIPO) (2001). "Geographical indications: historical background, nature of rights, existing systems for protection and obtaining effective protection in other countries," prepared for the Standing Committee on the Law of Trademarks, Industrial Designs and Geographical Indications, sixth session, Geneva, 12-16 March (SCT/6/3).

_____ (2003). "Economic importance of trademarks and geographical indications and their use in commerce", background document, accessed from www.wipo.int/meetings/es/html.jsp?url=http://www.wipo.int/arab/en/meetings/2003/tm_bey/doc/wipo_tm_bey_03_3.doc.

World Trade Organization (WTO) (2001a). Communication on "Work on issues relevant to the protection of geographical indications: extension of the protection of geographical indications for wines and spirits to geographical indications for other products" (IP/C/W/308/Rev.1).

_____ (2001b). Proposal on "Work on issues relevant to the protection of geographical indications: extension of the protection of geographical indications for wines and spirits to geographical indications for other products" (IP/C/W/247).

_____ (2002). Communication on "The extension of the additional protection for geographical indications to products other than wines and spirits" (IP/C/W/353).

_____ (2008). Communication on "Doha work programme–the extension of the additional protection for geographical indications to products other than wines and spirits" (TN/C/W/48).

MEASURING THE IMPACT OF CASH CROPS ON HOUSEHOLD EXPENDITURE AND POVERTY IN RURAL VIET NAM

Nguyen Viet Cuong*

This paper measures the impacts of cash crops on household consumption expenditure and poverty in rural Viet Nam using data from the Viet Nam household living standards surveys (VHLSSs) of 2002 and 2004. It has been found that revenues from cash crops have positive and statistically significant impacts on per capita expenditure. More specifically, an increase of 1 Viet Nam dong (VND) in rice revenues leads to an increase of 0.019 VND in per capita expenditure, and the corresponding figures for revenues from annual crops, perennial crops and fruits are 0.038, 0.040 and 0.036, respectively. As a result, crop sales have positive and statistically significant impacts on poverty reduction for crop-growing households and the rural population. The poverty-reducing impacts are found to be positive for all three Foster-Greer-Thorbecke poverty measures.

I. INTRODUCTION

It is often argued that crop production has an important role in economic development and poverty reduction. Crop production can contribute to economic growth through different channels, such as the provision of food and employment generation (e.g., see Johnston and Mellor 1961; Ranis and others 1990; Irz and others 2001; Timmer 2002). Agricultural growth can result in a remarkable reduction in poverty (Thorbecke and Jung 1996). Together with the trade liberalization trend, it can bring important sources of income from exportation.[1]

However, when integrated into the global economy, the crop sector of a country can be adversely affected by global economic shocks. A channel for shock transmission is the price of output and inputs (Winters and others 2004; Easterly and Kraay 2000). A sudden decrease in the price of crop outputs can quickly push the poor households who produce crops into losses and poverty. Coffee growing in Viet Nam is an example. In the late 1990s, the price of coffee was very high in the world market, and many households in Tay Nguyen Province grew coffee. However, afterwards the price of coffee suddenly dropped, and this affected many households as 80 per cent of the poor households grew coffee in Tay Nguyen (World Bank 2004). The farmers often bought production inputs with delayed payments, and as the coffee price fell, they became indebted, and had to sell their land to pay the debts. Another example is the harmful impact of the reduction in the price of corn in Mexico. Poor farmers could not respond to decreases in the price of corn and they suffered from losses

---

* Lecturer, Faculty of Trade and International Economics, National Economics University, Viet Nam.

[1] The role of trade liberalization is discussed in numerous studies, e.g., Harrison (2005), Winters and others (2004), and McCulloch and others (2001).

in incomes from corn production (Levy and Wijnbergen 1992; Nadal 2000). As a result, the effect of a decrease in crop prices on poverty reduction is not assumed to be always positive.

In addition, the industry and service sectors tend to grow more quickly than the agricultural sector in the long run. The shrinking of agriculture relative to industry and services has been observed in both developed and developing countries. Non-farm employment and business have proved to be an effective way to increase household income and reduce poverty (e.g., Lanjouw and Lanjouw 1995; Lanjouw 1998; Van de Walle 1994; Ruerd and van den Berg 2001).

Viet Nam has been an agricultural country, with about 60 per cent of the population involved in crop production in 2006. It is also a leading country in exporting rice, coffee and tea. The export value of agricultural products increased from 24,500 billion VND to 100,200 billion VND during the period 1995-2006.[2] However, the share of crop products in total export revenues dropped from 32 to 14 per cent during this period. It is not clear whether cash crops still make an important contribution to household consumption and poverty reduction. The main objective of this paper is to measure the impacts of household sales of different crops on per capita expenditure and poverty reduction. Information from the study can be helpful for policymakers in designing programmes and policies related to crop production. Data used in this paper are from the Viet Nam household living standards surveys (VHLSSs) of 2002 and 2004.

There are six sections of this paper. The second section describes data sources used for this paper, and the third section gives a brief overview of cash crop production and household welfare in Viet Nam. Next, the fourth section presents a methodology of the impact evaluation of crop sales. The fifth section presents empirical findings on impact estimation. Finally, the sixth section provides a conclusion.

II. DATA SET

This study relies on data from the two recent VHLSSs, which were conducted in 2002 and 2004 by the General Statistics Office of Viet Nam with technical support from the World Bank. The VHLSSs covered 30,000 and 9,000 households, respectively.

The samples are representative of the national and regional, rural and urban, levels. It should be noted that the General Statistics Office increased the sample size of the 2002 VHLSS to 30,000 households so that the data could be representative of some large provinces. However, this large sample survey was very expensive, and the sample size of VHLSS 2004 was reduced to 9,000 households. The 2002 and 2004 VHLSSs set up a panel of 4,000 households, which were representative of the whole country, for both the urban and rural populations.

---

[2] $1 was approximately 16,000 VND in January 2006.

The surveys collected information through household and community level questionnaires. Information on households included basic demography, employment and labour force participation, education, health, income, expenditure, housing, fixed assets and durable goods, and the participation of households in poverty alleviation programmes.

In VHLSSs, expenditure and income per capita are collected using very detailed questionnaires. Expenditure includes food and non-food expenses. Food expenditure includes purchased food and foodstuffs, and self-produced products of households. Non-food expenditure comprises spending on education, health care, houses and commodities, and on power, water and garbage removal. Regarding income, household income can come from any source, and includes income from agricultural and non-agricultural production, salaries, wages, pensions, scholarships, income from loan interest and house rentals, remittances and social transfers. Income from agricultural production comprises crop income, livestock income, aquaculture income, and income from other agriculture-related activities.

Information on commune characteristics was collected from 2,960 and 2,181 communes in the 2002 and 2004 surveys, respectively. Data on commune characteristics consist of demography and the general situation of communes, general economic conditions and aid programmes, non-farm employment, agriculture production, local infrastructure and transportation, education, health and social affairs. Commune data can be linked with household data. However, the commune data in the 2004 VHLSS are only available for rural areas.

This study focuses on the rural population. The main reason is that commune variables are used in regression analysis of the transfer impact, and there are only data on commune variables for rural areas in the 2004 VHLSS. In addition, poverty in Viet Nam is mostly a rural phenomenon, with 95 per cent of all poor living in rural areas in 2004. The number of households in the rural panel for 2002-2004 is 3,099.

III. CASH CROP PRODUCTION AND HOUSEHOLD WELFARE IN VIET NAM

In this paper, cash crops are defined as crops that households grow for sale. They consist of rice, industrial perennial crops (rubber, coffee, tea, peanuts, cashew nuts and peppers), fruits and annual crops. Annual crops include sugar cane, vegetables, potatoes, maize and others. The value of cash crops increased at an annual growth rate of 6 per cent during the period 1995-2006. However, there is evidence that the agricultural sector is shrinking. Figure 1 presents the share of the crop value in gross domestic product (GDP) over time. It shows that this share was decreased from 23 to 15 per cent during the period 1995-2006.

Figure 1. Share of the crop value in GDP

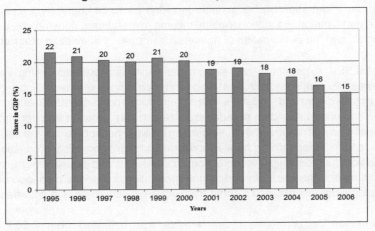

Source: Statistical yearbooks of the General Statistics Office of Viet Nam.

In addition, the share of agricultural products of total export revenues was reduced more quickly. Figure 2 shows that this share decreased from 32 per cent in 1995 to 14 per cent in 2006.

Figure 2. Crop exports share of total export revenues

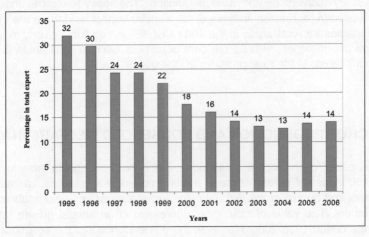

Source: Statistical yearbooks of the General Statistics Office of Viet Nam.

Although the share of agriculture of GDP tends to decrease over time, the proportion of households involved in agriculture remains rather high in rural Viet Nam. Figure 3 presents the percentage of rural households producing cash crops in the period 2002-2004. It shows that the ratio of households producing cash crops increased from 69 to 72 per cent. The proportion of households producing each crop type also increased. It should be noted that the proportion of households producing all crops was larger than the proportion of households producing cash crops (crops for sale), since there were households growing crops for consumption. The proportion of households producing crops in rural areas decreased slightly from 82 to 81 per cent during the period 2002-2004.

Figure 3. Percentage of households producing cash crops

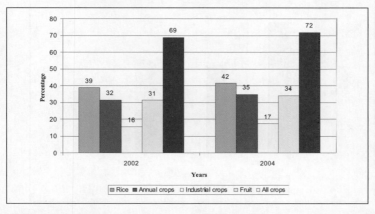

Source: Estimations from the Viet Nam household living standards surveys of 2002 and 2004.

Households without cash crops tended to have a higher consumption expenditure and lower poverty than those with cash crops (figures 4 and 5). Among the cash crop households, households with industrial crops experienced the highest expenditure growth rate during 2002-2004.

Figure 4. Per capita expenditure of households with and without cash crops

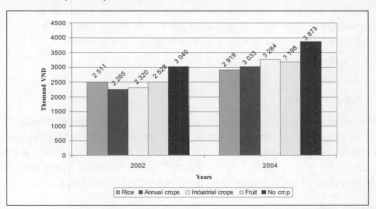

Source: Estimations from the Viet Nam household living standards surveys of 2002 and 2004.

All the household groups had experienced poverty reduction during the period 2002-2004. Households with rice sales had the lowest poverty incidence compared with households with other crops (annual and industrial crops). Meanwhile, households with industrial crops had the highest poverty incidence.

Figure 5. Poverty incidence of households with and without cash crops (percentage)

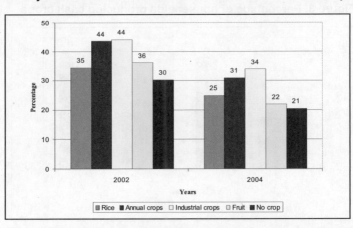

Source: Estimations from the Viet Nam household living standards surveys of 2002 and 2004.

IV. METHODS OF IMPACT MEASUREMENT

Impact on household consumption expenditure

This section presents the method for measuring the impacts of crop sales on household consumption expenditure and poverty. In this paper, expenditure is assumed to be a linear and a semi-log linear function of household characteristics:

$$Y_i = \alpha + X_i\beta + D_i\gamma + \varepsilon_i, \tag{1}$$

$$\ln(Y_i) = \alpha + X_i\beta + D_i\gamma + \varepsilon_i, \tag{2}$$

where Y_i is the per capita expenditure of household I, X_i are household characteristics, and D_i is a vector of revenues of crops, including rice, annual crops, industrial crops and fruit crops from crop-growing households. It should be noted that crop revenues are money that households obtain from crop sales.[3] The impact of D is estimated using both functions to examine the sensitivity of impact estimates to different functions of outcome.[4]

---

[3] Income is defined as revenues minus costs.

[4] We do not use the double-log function, i.e., $\ln(Y_i) = \alpha + X_i\beta + \ln(D_i)\gamma + \varepsilon_i$, since for households without crops, we get missing values of $\ln(D_i)$.

Since D is a continuous variable, one is often interested in the marginal effect (ME), which is the derivative of Y with respect to D. For equations (1) and (2), respectively, ME is equal to:

$$ME = \frac{\partial Y}{\partial D} = \gamma , \tag{3}$$

$$ME = \frac{\partial Y}{\partial D} = e^{(\alpha + X_i \beta + D_i \gamma + \varepsilon_i)}(\gamma) = Y_i \gamma . \tag{4}$$

Since ME in the semi-log function of outcome varies across the outcome value, one can use the average partial effect to measure the impact of D (Wooldridge 2001). In this paper, we define the average partial effect on the treated (APET), which measures how the average impact on crop-selling households changes due to a small change in crop revenues.

In the case of equation (1), APET is equal to ME, and it is estimated by $\hat{\gamma}$. In the case of equation (2), APET is expressed as follows:

$$APET = E\left(\frac{\partial Y}{\partial D}\bigg|D > 0\right) = E(Y_i \gamma \mid D_i > 0). \tag{5}$$

Thus the estimator is given by:

$$A\hat{P}ET = \frac{1}{n_p} \sum_{i=1}^{n_p} (Y_i \hat{\gamma}), \tag{6}$$

where n_p is the number of crop-selling households. The standard error of the estimates is calculated using a bootstrap technique.

The difficulty in estimating the effect of crop sales is the endogeneity of the crop sales. Unobserved variables, such as working conditions, production and business skills, and information, can be correlated with the crop sales. This paper uses instrumental-variables regressions and fixed-effect regressions to correct for the endogeneity of crop sales in the expenditure equation.

Impact on poverty

In this paper, poverty is measured by three Foster-Greer-Thorbecke poverty indexes, which can all be calculated using the following formula (Foster, Greer and Thorbecke 1984):

$$P_\alpha = \frac{1}{n} \sum_{i=1}^{q} \left[\frac{z - Y_i}{z}\right]^\alpha , \tag{7}$$

where Y_i is a welfare indicator (consumption expenditure per capita in this paper) for person i, z is the poverty line, n is the number of people in the sample population, q is the number of poor people, and α can be interpreted as a measure of inequality aversion.

When $\alpha = 0$, we have the headcount index H, which measures the proportion of people below the poverty line. When $\alpha = 1$ and $\alpha = 2$, we have the poverty gap PG, which measures the depth of poverty, and the squared poverty gap P_2, which measures the severity of poverty, respectively.

The impact of crop sales on the index of poverty of the recipients is expressed as follows:

$$\Delta P = P(D > 0, Y) - P(D > 0, Y_{(D=0)}),\tag{8}$$

where the first term on the left-hand side of (8) is the poverty measurement of the crop-selling households in the presence of crop revenues. This term is observed and can be estimated directly from the sample data. However, the second term on the right-hand side of (8) is the counterfactual measurement of poverty, i.e., the poverty indexes of crop-selling households if they had not sold the crops. This term is not observed directly, and it is estimated for household i using the following predicted expenditure:

$$\hat{Y}_{i(D_i=0)} \mid D_i > 0 = Y_i - \hat{\gamma}D_i,\tag{9}$$

Where $\hat{\gamma}$ is estimated from equation (1). In the case of equation (2), expenditure without crop revenues for crop-selling households is predicted as follows:

$$
\begin{aligned}
\hat{Y}_{i(D_i=0)} \mid D_i > 0 &= e^{\hat{\ln}(Y_{i(D=0)})} \\
&= e^{\hat{\alpha}+X_i\hat{\beta}+\hat{\varepsilon}_i} \\
&= e^{\hat{\alpha}+X_i\hat{\beta}+D_i\hat{\gamma}+\hat{\varepsilon}_i-D_i\hat{\gamma}} \\
&= e^{\ln(Y_i)-D_i\hat{\gamma}} \\
&= Y_i e^{-D_i\hat{\gamma}}.
\end{aligned}\tag{10}
$$

We can also measure the impact of crop sales on the total rural poverty as follows:

$$\Delta P = P(Y) - P(Y_{(D=0)}),\tag{11}$$

where $P(Y)$ is the observed poverty index of all the rural population (in which crop-selling households had crop sales), and $P(Y_{(D=0)})$ is the poverty index of all the rural population if crop-selling households had not received any money from crop sales.

V. EMPIRICAL RESULTS ON IMPACT MEASUREMENTS

In order to measure the impact of cash crops, the models of per capita expenditure are estimated using VHLSSs 2002 and 2004. The explanatory variables include household composition, the age of household head, the education of household head and household head's spouse, land and housing characteristics, regional dummy variables and commune characteristics. The list of explanatory variables is presented in table A.1 in the appendix.

In order to control for inflation, we have deflated all variables in terms of 2004 prices. To examine the sensitivity of impact estimates to different models, we use eight models (table A.2 in the appendix). Models 1 to 4 use the linear function of expenditure, while models 5 to 8 use the semi-log linear function of expenditure. For both outcome functions, there are four methods of estimation: fixed-effect and random-effect regressions using panel data from the 2002-2004 VHLSSs, ordinary least squares (OLS) regression using the 2004 VHLSS, and instrumental variable (IV) regression using the 2004 VHLSS. For the instrumental variable regression, the instrumental variables used for the crop revenues in 2004 are the revenues of cash crops in 2002. Although the validity of these instrumental variables can be questionable, empirical studies often use treatment variables in the past as instruments for the current treatment variables (e.g., see Van de Walle 2004).

The regression results reported in table A.2 in the appendix show that the estimates are stable across the models. The estimates of all the crop revenues are statistically significant in all the models. The R-squared is higher in the semi-log equations than in the linear function. The estimates of the coefficients of crop sales are also more statistically significant in the semi-log equations.

Using the instrumental variable regression, we can test the endogeneity of crop sales. Results from Durbin-Wu-Hausman tests show that the hypothesis on the exogeneity of crop sales is not rejected (table A.2 in the appendix). A problem in the instrumental variable regression is that the assumption on the exclusion of the instruments in the outcome equations might not be valid, since the sales in 2002 (the instruments) can affect household expenditure in 2004. Regarding the random-effect and fixed-effect models, the Hausman statistic that tests the null hypothesis of no systematic difference in coefficient estimates between two models is equal to 67.2 (result not reported in the paper). Thus, the null hypothesis is strongly rejected, and we incline to the fixed-effect model. In the following tables, only estimation results from models 1 and 5 (i.e., fixed-effect regressions) are reported. The estimation results from other models are quite similar and are not reported in this paper.[5]

Table 1 presents the estimates of APET for cash crop sales. All the estimates are positive and statistically significant. For example, model 5 shows that an increase of 1 VND in rice revenues leads to an increase of 0.019 VND in per capita expenditure. The corresponding figures for the sales of annual crops, perennial crops and fruits are 0.038, 0.040 and 0.036, respectively.

---

[5] These results can be provided on request.

Table 1. Impact of crop revenues on per capita expenditure

	Model 1	Model 5
Revenues of rice (thousand VND)	0.023*	0.019**
	[0.013]	[0.008]
Revenues of other annual crops (thousand VND)	0.030**	0.038***
	[0.013]	[0.013]
Revenues of perennial crops (thousand VND)	0.035***	0.040***
	[0.011]	[0.010]
Revenues of fruit (thousand VND)	0.039***	0.036***
	[0.015]	[0.013]

Source: Estimations from the Viet Nam household living standards surveys of 2002 and 2004.
Note: * significant at 10%, ** significant at 5%, *** significant at 1%.
Figures in parentheses are standard errors. Standard errors are corrected for sampling weights and estimated using bootstrap (non-parametric) with 200 replications.

Since cash crops have increased household expenditure, they can reduce the poverty of crop-selling households. In this paper, a household is classified as poor if their per capita expenditure is below the expenditure poverty line.[6] Tables 2 through 5 present the impact estimates on poverty of sales from rice, annual crops, perennial crops and fruits.

In table 2, estimates from model 1 are not statistically significant, while estimates from model 5 are statistically significant at the 5 per cent level. According to model 5, rice sales reduce the poverty incidence of the rice-growing households by about 1.4 percentage points. They also decrease the poverty gap and severity indexes by about 4.5 per cent. The effects on total poverty are smaller. Rice sales help to reduce the poverty incidence of all rural households by about 0.6 percentage points, and decrease the rural poverty gap and severity indexes by about 2 per cent.

---

[13] This poverty line was set up by the World Bank and the General Statistics Office. The poverty line is equivalent to the expenditure level that allows for nutritional needs and some essential non-food consumption, such as clothing and housing. This poverty line was first estimated in 1993. Poverty lines in the following years are estimated by deflating the 1993 poverty line using the consumer price index. Thus, the poverty lines are comparable over time. The poverty lines in the years 1993, 1998, 2002 and 2004 are equal to 1,160, 1,790, 1,917 and 2,077 thousand VND, respectively.

Table 2. Impact of rice sales on poverty

Index	With crop sales	Model 1		Model 5	
		Without crop sales	Impact	Without crop sales	Impact
Poverty of recipients					
Poverty incidence (P0)	0.2534***	0.2731***	-0.0197	0.2671***	-0.0137**
	[0.0144]	[0.0217]	[0.0176]	[0.0145]	[0.0070]
Poverty gap index (P1)	0.0630***	0.0713***	-0.0083	0.0661***	-0.0031**
	[0.0048]	[0.0080]	[0.0061]	[0.0050]	[0.0014]
Poverty severity index (P2)	0.0227***	0.0266***	-0.0039	0.0238***	-0.0011**
	[0.0023]	[0.0046]	[0.0037]	[0.0025]	[0.0005]
Poverty of the rural population					
Poverty incidence (P0)	0.2540***	0.2624***	-0.0084	0.2598***	-0.0059**
	[0.0085]	[0.0118]	[0.0076]	[0.0090]	[0.0030]
Poverty gap index (P1)	0.0611***	0.0646***	-0.0036	0.0624***	-0.0013**
	[0.0026]	[0.0039]	[0.0026]	[0.0030]	[0.0006]
Poverty severity index (P2)	0.0218***	0.0235***	-0.0017	0.0223***	-0.0005**
	[0.0012]	[0.0022]	[0.0016]	[0.0014]	[0.0002]

Source: Estimations from the Viet Nam household living standards surveys of 2002 and 2004.
Note: * significant at 10%, ** significant at 5%, *** significant at 1%.
Figures in parentheses are standard errors. Standard errors are corrected for sampling weights and estimated using bootstrap (non-parametric) with 200 replications.

Tables 3 and 4 present the impact estimates on poverty indexes of annual and perennial crop sales. All the estimates are statistically significant. Sales from annual and perennial crops reduce the poverty incidence of crop-growing households by 2.6 per cent (table 3) and 5.2 (table 4) percentage points (model 5). They also decrease the poverty gap and severity indexes of the crop-growing households and rural households. The effect of perennial crops is higher than that of annual crops. They reduce the poverty gap and severity indexes of the perennial-crop-growing households by approximately 12 per cent and 4 per cent (table 4), respectively.

Table 3. Impact of annual crop sales on poverty

Index	With crop sales	Model 1		Model 5	
		Without crop sales	Impact	Without crop sales	Impact
Poverty of recipients					
Poverty incidence (P0)	0.3102***	0.3394***	-0.0292***	0.3364***	-0.0262***
	[0.0157]	[0.0177]	[0.0094]	[0.0149]	[0.0077]
Poverty gap index (P1)	0.0823***	0.0941***	-0.0118**	0.0889***	-0.0065***
	[0.0053]	[0.0075]	[0.0048]	[0.0053]	[0.0022]
Poverty severity index (P2)	0.0315***	0.0381***	-0.0066**	0.0342***	-0.0027**
	[0.0028]	[0.0046]	[0.0034]	[0.0028]	[0.0010]
Poverty of the rural population					
Poverty incidence (P0)	0.2540***	0.2649***	-0.0109**	0.2638***	-0.0098***
	[0.0085]	[0.0102]	[0.0036]	[0.0087]	[0.0029]
Poverty gap index (P1)	0.0611***	0.0655***	-0.0044**	0.0635***	-0.0025***
	[0.0026]	[0.0038]	[0.0018]	[0.0027]	[0.0008]
Poverty severity index (P2)	0.0218***	0.0243***	-0.0025**	0.0228***	-0.0010**
	[0.0012]	[0.0021]	[0.0013]	[0.0013]	[0.0004]

Source: Estimations from the Viet Nam household living standards surveys of 2002 and 2004.

Note: * significant at 10%, ** significant at 5%, *** significant at 1%.

Figures in parentheses are standard errors. Standard errors are corrected for sampling weights and estimated using bootstrap (non-parametric) with 200 replications.

Table 4. Impact of perennial crop sales on poverty

Index	With crop sales	Model 1		Model 5	
		Without crop sales	Impact	Without crop sales	Impact
Poverty of recipients					
Poverty incidence (P0)	0.3370***	0.4087***	-0.0717***	0.3889***	-0.0520***
	[0.0222]	[0.0287]	[0.0202]	[0.0268]	[0.0153]
Poverty gap index (P1)	0.0795***	0.1103***	-0.0308**	0.0912***	-0.0117***
	[0.0069]	[0.0185]	[0.0160]	[0.0088]	[0.0043]
Poverty severity index (P2)	0.0271***	0.0431***	-0.0160	0.0314***	-0.0042**
	[0.0031]	[0.0178]	[0.0172]	[0.0039]	[0.0018]
Poverty of the rural population					
Poverty incidence (P0)	0.2540***	0.2676***	-0.0136***	0.2638***	-0.0099***
	[0.0085]	[0.0094]	[0.0039]	[0.0091]	[0.0029]
Poverty gap index (P1)	0.0611***	0.0669***	-0.0058**	0.0633***	-0.0022***
	[0.0026]	[0.0044]	[0.0032]	[0.0030]	[0.0008]
Poverty severity index (P2)	0.0218***	0.0249***	-0.0030	0.0226***	-0.0008***
	[0.0012]	[0.0037]	[0.0033]	[0.0015]	[0.0003]

Source: Estimations from the Viet Nam household living standards surveys of 2002 and 2004.
Note: * significant at 10%, ** significant at 5%, *** significant at 1%.
Figures in parentheses are standard errors. Standard errors are corrected for sampling weights and estimated using bootstrap (non-parametric) with 200 replications.

Finally, table 5 reports impact estimates of fruit sales. Fruit sales decrease the poverty rate of growing households by about 1.1 percentage points (model 5). The estimated effect on the poverty rate of rural households is quite small, at 0.4 percentage points. Regarding poverty gap and severity, most of the estimates are not statistically significant. This might be because the poverty gap and indexes of the fruit-growing households are smaller than those of households with other crops.

Table 5. Impact of fruit sales on poverty

Index	With crop sales	Model 1		Model 5	
		Without crop sales	Impact	Without crop sales	Impact
Poverty of recipients					
Poverty incidence (P0)	0.2162***	0.2373***	-0.0210**	0.2267***	-0.0105**
	[0.0120]	[0.0158]	[0.0095]	[0.0153]	[0.0051]
Poverty gap index (P1)	0.0475***	0.0525***	-0.0049	0.0499***	-0.0023**
	[0.0039]	[0.0057]	[0.0039]	[0.0047]	[0.0009]
Poverty severity index (P2)	0.0163***	0.0185***	-0.0021	0.0167***	-0.0003
	[0.0020]	[0.0044]	[0.0039]	[0.0023]	[0.0003]
Poverty of the rural population					
Poverty incidence (P0)	0.2540***	0.2615***	-0.0076**	0.2580***	-0.0041**
	[0.0076]	[0.0088]	[0.0034]	[0.0090]	[0.0018]
Poverty gap index (P1)	0.0611***	0.0628***	-0.0018	0.0615***	-0.0005
	[0.0027]	[0.0032]	[0.0014]	[0.0028]	[0.0003]
Poverty severity index (P2)	0.0218***	0.0226***	-0.0008	0.0219***	-0.0001
	[0.0013]	[0.0020]	[0.0014]	[0.0013]	[0.0001]

Source: Estimations from the Viet Nam household living standards surveys of 2002 and 2004.
Note: * significant at 10%, ** significant at 5%, *** significant at 1%.
Figures in parentheses are standard errors. Standard errors are corrected for sampling weights and estimated using bootstrap (non-parametric) with 200 replications.

It should be noted that the impact of cash crop revenues on expenditure and poverty is measured by comparing expenditure and poverty in the presence of crop revenues and counterfactual expenditure and poverty in the absence of crop revenues. Expenditure and poverty are not compared between crop households and non-crop households. Although households with crops tend to have lower expenditure and higher poverty than households without crops, crop revenues still play an important role in increasing expenditure and reducing poverty for the crop-growing households. This is because crop revenues are still a main revenue source for crop-growing households.

VI. CONCLUSION

Viet Nam is a developing country with a large proportion of the population involved in agricultural activities. Although crop production is often named as an important activity for economic growth and poverty reduction, there are only a few studies measuring the quantitative impacts of crop production on poverty reduction. This paper is the first study that uses nationally representative household surveys in order to measure the impacts of cash crop sales on household consumption expenditure and poverty in Viet Nam.

It has been found that revenues from cash crops have positive and statistically significant impacts on the per capita expenditure of crop-selling households. More specifically, an increase of 1 VND in rice revenues leads to an increase of 0.019 VND in per capita expenditure, and the corresponding figures for sales of annual crops, perennial crops, and fruits are 0.038, 0.040 and 0.036, respectively. As a result, the crop sales help reduce poverty of the crop-growing households and rural population. Among the crops, perennial crops have largest effect on poverty reduction in terms of point estimates. They decrease the poverty incidence of the crop-growing households by approximately 5.2 percentage points. They reduce the poverty gap and severity indexes of the perennial-crop-growing households by about 12 per cent. The fruit crop sales have small point estimates of impacts on poverty. They decrease the poverty rate of the growing households and all rural household by about 1.1 and 0.4 percentage points, respectively.

The findings might suggest several policy implications for crop production in Viet Nam. First, non-farm production can be an important activity for increasing income, expenditure and reducing poverty. Descriptive data analysis shows that households with crops tend to have lower expenditure and higher poverty than households without crops. Second, cash crops still have an important role in poverty reduction, and the Government should have measures and policies to increase the crop revenues of farm households. The findings also show that perennial crops have a greater effect on poverty reduction than other crops. Thus, the promotion of perennial crops can result in a remarkable reduction in rural poverty.

ANNEX

Table A.1. Variable description

Variables	Type	2002		2004	
		Mean	Standard deviation	Mean	Standard deviation
Per capita expenditure (thousand VND)*	Continuous	2 839.6	40.1	3 340.4	46.0
Variables of crop sales					
Revenues of rice (thousand VND)*	Continuous	2 330.3	214.1	2 687.7	207.1
Revenues of annual crops (thousand VND)*	Continuous	604.4	56.4	984.6	91.1
Revenues of perennial crops (thousand VND)*	Continuous	848.6	158.9	1 295.0	220.2
Revenues of fruit (thousand VND)*	Continuous	855.4	107.9	898.0	100.9
Household variables					
Ratio of members younger than 16 years	Continuous	0.305	0.005	0.280	0.004
Ratio of members older than 60 years	Continuous	0.089	0.003	0.095	0.003
Age of household head	Discrete	47.0	0.3	48.4	0.3
Household size	Discrete	5.061	0.044	5.133	0.049
Head with less than primary school	Binary	0.341	0.011	0.316	0.011
Head with primary school	Binary	0.260	0.009	0.264	0.009
Head with lower secondary school	Binary	0.282	0.011	0.278	0.010
Head with upper secondary school	Binary	0.070	0.005	0.055	0.005
Head with technical degree	Binary	0.036	0.004	0.070	0.005
Head with post secondary school	Binary	0.011	0.002	0.017	0.003
Head with no spouse	Binary	0.137	0.007	0.140	0.007
Head's spouse with less than primary school	Binary	0.334	0.012	0.323	0.011
Head's spouse with primary school	Binary	0.228	0.009	0.229	0.009
Head's spouse with lower secondary school	Binary	0.231	0.010	0.224	0.010
Head's spouse with upper secondary school	Binary	0.043	0.004	0.037	0.004
Head's spouse with technical degree	Binary	0.017	0.003	0.036	0.004
Head's spouse with post secondary school	Binary	0.010	0.002	0.010	0.002
Log of living areas (log of m²)	Continuous	3.902	0.012	3.981	0.012

Table A.1. Variable description *(continued)*

Variables	Type	2002		2004	
		Mean	Standard deviation	Mean	Standard deviation
Living in permanent house	Binary	0.117	0.008	0.136	0.008
Living in semi-permanent house	Binary	0.603	0.012	0.624	0.011
Living in temporary house	Binary	0.279	0.011	0.239	0.011
Area of annual crop land (m²)	Continuous	4 305.1	203.5	4 374.7	195.6
Area of perennial crop land (m²)	Continuous	1 532.7	141.5	1 248.8	139.5
Area of forestry land (m²)	Continuous	1 666.1	296.9	1 144.8	191.8
Area of aquaculture water surface (m²)	Continuous	399.7	84.7	316.6	70.1
Commune variables					
Having non-farm enterprise in commune	Binary	0.979	0.005	0.841	0.012
Distance to nearest town (km)	Continuous	8.785	0.283	9.158	0.309
Distance to nearest road (km)	Continuous	0.684	0.099	0.594	0.099
Distance to nearest daily market (km)	Continuous	2.795	0.184	3.087	0.187
Distance to nearest periodic market (km)	Continuous	3.560	0.233	2.052	0.140
Distance to nearest post (km)	Continuous	3.091	0.192	2.361	0.152
Dummy regional variables					
Red River Delta	Binary	0.201	0.013	0.201	0.013
North East	Binary	0.129	0.010	0.129	0.010
North West	Binary	0.031	0.005	0.031	0.005
North Central Coast	Binary	0.152	0.013	0.152	0.013
South Central Coast	Binary	0.089	0.009	0.089	0.009
Central Highlands	Binary	0.063	0.008	0.063	0.008
North East South	Binary	0.094	0.009	0.094	0.009
Mekong River Delta	Binary	0.242	0.014	0.242	0.014
Number of observations		3 099		3 099	

Source: Estimations from Viet Nam household living standards surveys 2002 and 2004.

Note: * 2004 price.

Table A.2. Regression results

Explanatory variables	Dependent variable: Per capita expenditure				Dependent variable: Logarithm of per capita expenditure			
	Model 1: Fixed-effect	Model 2: Random effect	Model 3: OLS	Model 4: IV	Model 5: Fixed-effect	Model 6: Random effect	Model 7: OLS	Model 8: IV
Revenues of rice	0.023*	0.031***	0.034***	0.030***	0.0000043**	0.0000088***	0.0000083***	0.0000093***
	[0.013]	[0.007]	[0.009]	[0.010]	[0.0000020]	[0.0000012]	[0.0000012]	[0.0000019]
Revenues of annual crops	0.030**	0.023***	0.018**	0.025*	0.0000102***	0.0000091***	0.0000074***	0.0000103**
	[0.013]	[0.008]	[0.008]	[0.010]	[0.0000031]	[0.0000022]	[0.0000021]	[0.0000046]
Revenues of perennial crops	0.035***	0.023***	0.020***	0.024***	0.0000086***	0.0000055***	0.0000044***	0.0000051***
	[0.011]	[0.003]	[0.005]	[0.007]	[0.0000021]	[0.0000008]	[0.0000010]	[0.0000015]
Revenues of fruit	0.039***	0.040***	0.036***	0.035***	0.0000093***	0.0000116***	0.0000097***	0.0000106***
	[0.015]	[0.010]	[0.011]	[0.013]	[0.0000024]	[0.0000018]	[0.0000019]	[0.0000030]
Ratio of members younger than 16 years	-1 261.4***	-1 720.9***	-2 001.0***	-1 995.7***	-0.35524***	-0.50076***	-0.55623***	-0.55494***
	[277.9]	[150.4]	[190.3]	[189.0]	[0.06152]	[0.03625]	[0.04579]	[0.04559]
Ratio of members who older than 60	-1 225.4***	-1 104.0***	-1 063.6***	-1 080.8***	-0.27818***	-0.28503***	-0.26653***	-0.26530***
	[340.9]	[176.8]	[231.8]	[232.0]	[0.07231]	[0.03923]	[0.04931]	[0.04929]
Head age	67.319**	-0.669	-2.76	-2.534	0.02319***	0.00523	-0.00001	-0.00015
	[31.319]	[14.067]	[15.835]	[15.663]	[0.00793]	[0.00381]	[0.00424]	[0.00422]
Head age squared	-0.505*	0.085	0.081	0.083	-0.00018*	-0.00002	0.00002	0.00002
	[0.303]	[0.136]	[0.149]	[0.147]	[0.00008]	[0.00004]	[0.00004]	[0.00004]
Household size	-813.307***	-562.218***	-592.555***	-594.747***	-0.18473***	-0.13634***	-0.12364***	-0.12426***
	[109.723]	[63.408]	[78.441]	[78.030]	[0.02271]	[0.01324]	[0.01602]	[0.01596]

Table A.2. (continued)

Explanatory variables	Dependent variable: Per capita expenditure				Dependent variable: Logarithm of per capita expenditure			
	Model 1: Fixed-effect	Model 2: Random effect	Model 3: OLS	Model 4: IV	Model 5: Fixed-effect	Model 6: Random effect	Model 7: OLS	Model 8: IV
Household size squared	45.758***	25.554***	24.996***	24.915***	0.00860***	0.00464***	0.00323**	0.00329**
	[8.430]	[5.146]	[6.043]	[5.973]	[0.00187]	[0.00111]	[0.00134]	[0.00133]
Head with less than primary school	Omitted							
Head with primary school	199.253*	254.947***	253.845***	252.004***	0.04643**	0.08811***	0.09348***	0.09457***
	[110.781]	[62.640]	[94.990]	[94.831]	[0.02357]	[0.01557]	[0.02178]	[0.02175]
Head with lower secondary school	299.179**	404.695***	547.563***	547.180***	0.08099**	0.12412***	0.15533***	0.15729***
	[149.047]	[76.227]	[113.818]	[113.203]	[0.03273]	[0.01858]	[0.02491]	[0.02493]
Head with upper secondary school	260.563	518.121***	475.746***	476.868***	0.12790***	0.18150***	0.16949***	0.17103***
	[253.859]	[114.893]	[148.381]	[147.202]	[0.04928]	[0.02898]	[0.03606]	[0.03570]
Head with technical degree	881.8***	1 073.54***	1 061.94***	1 062.55***	0.23388***	0.29430***	0.29453***	0.29786***
	[207.90]	[141.93]	[180.17]	[179.03]	[0.04200]	[0.02882]	[0.03740]	[0.03729]
Head with post secondary school	1 055.29**	1 735.88***	1 873.94***	1 874.67***	0.26970***	0.43397***	0.46631***	0.46988***
	[490.660]	[280.295]	[314.350]	[313.048]	[0.07819]	[0.04646]	[0.05257]	[0.05234]
Head with no spouse	Omitted							

Table A.2. (continued)

Explanatory variables	Dependent variable: Per capita expenditure				Dependent variable: Logarithm of per capita expenditure			
	Model 1: Fixed-effect	Model 2: Random effect	Model 3: OLS	Model 4: IV	Model 5: Fixed-effect	Model 6: Random effect	Model 7: OLS	Model 8: IV
Head's spouse with less than primary school	-386.828*	-312.130***	-313.697***	-310.602***	-0.05797	-0.08579***	-0.09113***	-0.09265***
	[221.162]	[88.222]	[115.865]	[114.872]	[0.04497]	[0.02102]	[0.02535]	[0.02533]
Head's spouse with primary school	-366.332	-152.198	-107.205	-104.212	-0.03685	-0.01672	-0.00898	-0.01201
	[234.085]	[101.092]	[132.681]	[131.098]	[0.04565]	[0.02317]	[0.02840]	[0.02850]
Head's spouse with lower secondary school	-325.632	-362.411***	-510.096***	-512.178***	-0.01596	-0.05061**	-0.09259***	-0.09412***
	[240.926]	[106.936]	[144.959]	[143.424]	[0.04947]	[0.02420]	[0.03048]	[0.03032]
Head's spouse with upper secondary school	-285.121	126.614	81.632	86.872	0.00537	0.06202	0.03807	0.03667
	[379.955]	[172.244]	[253.240]	[251.963]	[0.07318]	[0.03805]	[0.05078]	[0.05057]
Head's spouse with technical degree	572.955	884.202***	715.544**	713.291**	0.13973**	0.19583***	0.16427***	0.16285***
	[418.545]	[310.969]	[313.438]	[312.271]	[0.06998]	[0.04105]	[0.04549]	[0.04530]
Head's spouse with post secondary school	593.67	1 200.40***	1 327.12***	1 326.61***	0.20749**	0.28664***	0.27745***	0.27808***
	[595.691]	[348.851]	[424.874]	[422.373]	[0.09514]	[0.05953]	[0.06711]	[0.06690]

Table A.2. (continued)

Explanatory variables	Dependent variable: Per capita expenditure				Dependent variable: Logarithm of per capita expenditure			
	Model 1: Fixed-effect	Model 2: Random effect	Model 3: OLS	Model 4: IV	Model 5: Fixed-effect	Model 6: Random effect	Model 7: OLS	Model 8: IV
Log of living areas (log of m²)	368.599***	751.248***	968.838***	975.854***	0.08287***	0.18655***	0.24961***	0.24795***
	[82.784]	[68.084]	[104.766]	[105.512]	[0.01780]	[0.01596]	[0.02289]	[0.02281]
Living in permanent house	705.865***	742.172***	780.790***	775.023***	0.16731***	0.20322***	0.20782***	0.20724***
	[156.135]	[100.190]	[143.871]	[143.318]	[0.03104]	[0.02181]	[0.03048]	[0.03036]
Living in semi-permanent house	192.595**	248.010***	237.497***	233.312***	0.06663***	0.09793***	0.09949***	0.09935***
	[78.723]	[48.789]	[79.680]	[79.565]	[0.01873]	[0.01396]	[0.02086]	[0.02082]
Living in temporary house	Omitted							
Area of annual crop land (m²)	0.006	-0.004	0.004	0.006	0.0000022	-0.0000012	0.0000011	0.0000002
	[0.009]	[0.005]	[0.007]	[0.008]	[0.0000018]	[0.0000014]	[0.0000016]	[0.0000019]
Area of perennial crop land (m²)	0.002	0.010**	0.021***	0.018***	0.0000006	0.0000027**	0.0000052***	0.0000047***
	[0.006]	[0.005]	[0.005]	[0.007]	[0.0000013]	[0.0000012]	[0.0000012]	[0.0000014]
Forestry land (m²)	0.006**	-0.001	-0.003	-0.003	0.0000015*	-0.0000003	-0.0000011	-0.000001
	[0.003]	[0.002]	[0.003]	[0.003]	[0.0000009]	[0.0000005]	[0.0000007]	[0.0000007]
Area of aquaculture water surface (m²)	0.02	0.030***	0.017	0.017	0.0000043	0.0000096***	0.0000070**	0.0000070**
	[0.013]	[0.011]	[0.014]	[0.014]	[0.0000038]	[0.0000022]	[0.0000031]	[0.0000031]

Table A.2. (continued)

Explanatory variables	Dependent variable: Per capita expenditure				Dependent variable: Logarithm of per capita expenditure			
	Model 1: Fixed-effect	Model 2: Random effect	Model 3: OLS	Model 4: IV	Model 5: Fixed-effect	Model 6: Random effect	Model 7: OLS	Model 8: IV
Commune having non-farm activities	-185.442**	-198.540**	-41.603	-46.602	-0.06431***	-0.06598***	-0.02965	-0.02995
	[85.032]	[78.267]	[100.667]	[100.282]	[0.02027]	[0.01606]	[0.02288]	[0.02275]
Distance to nearest town (km)	1.276	-3.593	-8.955**	-9.100**	0.00107	-0.0006	-0.00234**	-0.00237**
	[4.047]	[2.869]	[4.229]	[4.245]	[0.00111]	[0.00083]	[0.00110]	[0.00109]
Distance to nearest road (km)	35.894	30.125***	34.730***	35.322***	0.00295	0.00642**	0.00890***	0.00885***
	[29.651]	[11.541]	[12.451]	[12.573]	[0.00519]	[0.00287]	[0.00299]	[0.00297]
Distance to nearest daily market (km)	7.328	-7.800**	-16.643**	-17.083**	0.00166	-0.00346***	-0.00930***	-0.00915***
	[6.072]	[3.733]	[6.826]	[6.677]	[0.00130]	[0.00099]	[0.00200]	[0.00197]
Distance to nearest periodic market (km)	-2.141	-2.531	-29.344***	-29.772***	-0.00067	-0.00103	-0.00756***	-0.00736***
	[4.787]	[4.077]	[7.426]	[7.498]	[0.00121]	[0.00099]	[0.00199]	[0.00199]
Distance to nearest post (km)	-10.523**	-14.368***	-17.676**	-17.985***	-0.00372***	-0.00501***	-0.00351*	-0.00364*
	[5.019]	[3.610]	[6.960]	[6.925]	[0.00135]	[0.00120]	[0.00193]	[0.00190]
Year 2008	451.777***	366.697***			0.12966***	0.10351***		
	[37.449]	[35.081]			[0.00931]	[0.00878]		
Red River Delta	Omitted							
North East		-189.344**	-323.409***	-343.437***		-0.06517**	-0.09394***	-0.09615***
		[92.510]	[112.082]	[113.021]		[0.02648]	[0.02924]	[0.02926]

Table A.2. (continued)

Explanatory variables	Dependent variable: Per capita expenditure				Dependent variable: Logarithm of per capita expenditure			
	Model 1: Fixed-effect	Model 2: Random effect	Model 3: OLS	Model 4: IV	Model 5: Fixed-effect	Model 6: Random effect	Model 7: OLS	Model 8: IV
North West		-299.428**	-136.261	-196.882		-0.18678***	-0.10716***	-0.11485***
		[123.520]	[172.881]	[177.290]		[0.04259]	[0.05222]	[0.05261]
North Central Coast		-200.129**	-302.910***	-316.375***		-0.08774***	-0.10776***	-0.10914***
		[83.708]	[105.745]	[105.541]		[0.02529]	[0.02913]	[0.02898]
South Central Coast		212.903**	174.441	153.874		0.06441**	0.0322	0.02996
		[100.582]	[130.848]	[129.647]		[0.02937]	[0.03383]	[0.03361]
Central Highlands		43.188	114.78	55.23		-0.06256*	-0.01886	-0.02795
		[118.826]	[167.408]	[176.044]		[0.03607]	[0.04667]	[0.04806]
North East South		1 321.041***	1 503.411***	1 507.550***		0.32822***	0.34042***	0.34022***
		[149.064]	[203.907]	[200.913]		[0.03248]	[0.03746]	[0.03719]
Mekong River Delta		775.163***	672.015***	749.269***		0.23169***	0.19538***	0.20387***
		[115.672]	[152.590]	[162.300]		[0.02742]	[0.03317]	[0.03551]
Constant	3 841.43***	1 977.73***	1 777.18***	1 677.43***	7.94997***	7.50379***	7.49063***	7.48028***
	[848.153]	[393.784]	[503.803]	[499.960]	[0.21306]	[0.10635]	[0.13217]	[0.13182]
Observations	6 198	6 198	3 099	3 099	6 198	6 198	3 099	3 099
Number of i	3 099	3 099			3 099	3 099		
R-squared	0.28	0.33	0.38		0.34	0.42	0.48	

Source: Estimations from the Viet Nam household living standards surveys of 2002 and 2004.

Note: Robust standard errors in brackets.

***, **, and * represent statistical significance at 1%, 5% and 10%, respectively.

The first stage regression in the IV regression is not reported. It can be provided on request.

Table A.3. Tests on weak instruments and underidentification of IV, and endogeneity of crop sales in IV regressions

	Per capita expenditure (model 4)	Logarithm of per capita expenditure (model 8)
Underidentification test of IV: Hansen J statistic	$X_{(1)} = 886.04$ P-value = 0.000	$X_{(1)} = 886.04$ P-value = 0.000
Test of endogeneity: Durbin-Wu-Hausman statistic	$X_{(1)} = 1.772$ P-value = 0.777	$X_{(1)} = 1.799$ P-value = 0.773
Weak IV identification test: Cragg-Donald F statistic	253.526	253.526

Source: Estimation from the 2004 Viet Nam household living standards survey.

REFERENCES

Easterly, W. and A. Kraay (2000). "Small states, small problems? Income, growth, and volatility in small states", *World Development*, vol. 28, No. 11, pp. 2013-2027.

Foster, J., J. Greer and E. Thorbecke (1984). "A class of decomposable poverty measures", *Econometrica*, vol. 52, pp. 761-765.

Harrison, A., ed. (2005). *Globalization and Poverty* (National Bureau of Economic Research Conference Report, Chicago University Press).

Irz, X., Lin Lin, C. Thirtle and S. Wiggins (2001). "Agricultural productivity growth and poverty alleviation", *Development Policy Review,* vol. 19, No. 4, pp. 449-466.

Johnston, B.F. and J.W. Mellor (1961). "The role of agriculture in economic development", *American Economic Review,* Vol. 51, pp. 566-593.

Lanjouw, J.O. and P. Lanjouw (1995). "Rural nonfarm employment: a survey", Policy Research Working Paper No. 1463 (World Bank).

Lanjouw, P. (1998). "Ecuador's rural nonfarm sector as a route out of poverty", Policy Research Working Paper No. 1094 (World Bank).

Levy, S. and S. van Wijnbergen (1992). "Agricultural adjustment and the Mexico-USA free trade agreement", in I. Goldin and L.A. Winters, eds., *Open Economies: Structural Adjustment and Agriculture* (Cambridge, Cambridge University Press), pp. 42-62.

McCulloch, N., L. A. Winters and X. Cirera (2001). *Trade Liberalization and Poverty: A Handbook* (London, Centre for Economic Policy Research).

Nadal, A. (2000). *The Environmental and Social Impacts of Economic Liberalization on Corn Production in Mexico* (Oxfam GB, and WWF International).

Ranis, G., F. Stewart, and E. Angeles-Reyes (1990). *Linkages in Developing Countries: A Philippine Study, ICS Press for International Center for Economic Growth* (San Francisco).

Ruerd, R. and M. van den Berg (2001). "Nonfarm employment and poverty alleviation of rural farm households in Honduras", *World Development*, vol. 29, No. 3, pp. 549-560.

Thorbecke, E. and H. Jung (1996). "A multiplier decomposition method to analyze poverty alleviation", *Journal of Development Economics,* vol. 48, pp. 279-300.

Timmer, C.P. (2002). "Agriculture and economic development", in B. Gardner and G. Rausser, eds., *Handbook of Agricultural Economics,* Vol. 2 (Elsevier Science B.V).

Van de Walle, D. (1994). "Rural poverty in an emerging market economy: is diversification into nonfarm activities in rural Viet Nam the solution?", Policy Research Department, World Bank, unpublished manuscript.

Van de Walle, D. (2004). "Testing Viet Nam's public safety net", *Journal of Comparative Economics*, vol. 32, No. 4, pp. 661-679.

Winters, A., N. McCulloch and A. McKay (2004). "Trade liberalization and poverty: the evidence so far", *Journal of Economic Literature*, Vol. XLII, pp. 72–115.

Wooldridge, J. M. (2001). *Econometric Analysis of Cross Section and Panel Data* (Cambridge, Massachusetts and London, MIT Press).

World Bank (2004). *Viet Nam Development Report: Poverty* (World Bank in Viet Nam).

ANALYSIS OF SAEMAUL UNDONG: A KOREAN RURAL DEVELOPMENT PROGRAMME IN THE 1970s

Sooyoung Park*

Saemaul Undong was a community-based integrated rural development programme of the Republic of Korea in the 1970s which contributed to narrowing the developmental gap between urban cities and rural communities over a decade. Its success can be attributed to its implementation of basic strategies of poverty reduction adapting to and making use of the Korean contexts—promoting opportunities and facilitating empowerment for rural people. Forty years ago, the people who designed and implemented Saemaul Undong did not have a clear understanding of the concepts and vocabularies that are broadly used in development today. What they promoted, achieved and implemented, however, was not different from the goals, objectives and methodologies that development practitioners promote today. The most important lesson learned from Saemaul Undong are that it devised appropriate strategies and measures reflecting and making use of the specific political, economic and social contexts. Developing countries should carefully study their own situation and devise workable and practical solutions of their own.

I. INTRODUCTION

Globally, more than 1.2 billion people are still living in extreme poverty on one dollar a day.[1] Though much progress has been made, reducing poverty remains a colossal task (World Bank 2000, p. 17). The case of the Republic of Korea in this circumstance is worth mentioning. The Republic of Korea has achieved remarkable socio-economic development and reduced extreme poverty, which had plagued the country for a very long time. Until now, it is the only country in the world that has overcome the three common hardships observed in most developing countries: civil wars or internal conflicts; a colonial legacy; and extreme poverty. In 1953, the per capita gross domestic product (GDP) of the Republic of Korea was $73, and this increased to $21,695 in 2007.[2] In 1965, 40.9 per cent of the population suffered from absolute poverty, but the poverty rate was reduced to 10.9 per cent by 2007.[3]

* Manager of the Evaluation Office, Korea International Cooperation Agency. This article was commissioned by ESCAP as part of the Regional Poverty Alleviation Programme: Replication of Best Practices in Rural Community Development (Saemaul Undong Phase II). The views and any conclusions reached in this article are those of the author and do not represent the policies of ESCAP or the Korea International Cooperation Agency.

[1] The level of extreme poverty was estimated by 1993 purchasing power parity.

[2] Bank of Korea Economic Statistics System, accessed from http://ecos.bok.or.kr.

[3] The 1965 poverty figure is from Sang-Mok Seo (1981). "Definition of poverty and time series analysis" pp. 27-28, accessed from www.kdi.re.kr/kdi/report/report_read05.jsp?pub_no=00003560 on March 21 2008; the 2007 poverty figure is from Myung-Jae Sung (2008). "Analysis on the impact of fiscal policy on Income distribution structure and poverty rate", *Monthly Public Finance Forum*, Korea Institute of Public Finance, No. 148, October, pp. 8-28.

Though its economic development policy focused on industrial development, the Republic of Korea effectively reduced rural as well as urban poverty. From 1970, the Government turned its attention towards balanced growth between urban cities and rural communities and within a decade managed to develop rural community conditions to match those of the cities. At the centre of this lies Saemaul Undong,[4] the integrated community development programme of the Republic of Korea.

This paper attempts to re-evaluate Saemaul Undong, focusing on its value as a rural development programme, identify what it really is and draw lessons applicable in current development practices. To do so, in the next chapter, the initiation, annual progress and results of Saemaul Undong will be explained, along with its objectives, outputs and outcomes. Based on this assessment, chapter three will draw some key factors of its success, and chapter four will identify some limitations and criticisms. Finally, chapter five will present some applicable lessons learned and implications of the programme for today's development contexts.

II. SAEMAUL UNDONG: PROGRESS AND RESULTS

It is very difficult to define Saemaul Undong due to the constant changes in its scope and agenda. If one focuses exclusively on activities performed in rural areas from 1970 to 1979, however, it is possible to find some common denominators shared throughout the entire movement. In short, Saemaul Undong was a community-based integrated rural development programme. As each Government of a developing country names its development programmes in its own way, Saemaul Undong was a brand name given by the Government of the Republic of Korea. Its success can be attributed to its implementation of basic strategies of poverty reduction adapting to and making use of the Korean contexts— promoting opportunities and facilitating empowerment for rural people. Forty years ago, the people who designed and implemented Saemaul Undong did not have a clear understanding of the concepts and vocabularies that are broadly used in development today, such as good governance, capacity-building, participatory approach, accountability, empowerment, vertical integration or ownership. In fact, some of these concepts did not even exist at that time. What they promoted, achieved and implemented, however, was not different from the goals, objectives and methodologies that development practitioners promote today.

---

[4] In a broad sense, Saemaul Undong, which can be translated as "new village movement" in English, was aimed not only at rural development but also, in its latter stages, at various enlightenment activities implemented in industrial factories, the military and cities. It is still maintained in some cities and villages under the administration of the privatized organization called the National Council of Saemaul Undong Movement in Korea. In general, Saemaul Undong is associated with rural development activities in the 1970s and many studies also confine their research scope accordingly. In this paper, Saemaul Undong refers only to the rural development activities and projects from 1970 to 1979 under President Park's regime before the privatization of the programme by the successive Government.

Initiation

The Government of the Republic of Korea achieved successful economic development in the 1970s with the adequate usage of selective industrial policies and export-oriented trade policies. This selective strategy, however, put rural development on hold and widened the gap between urban and rural living standards. Discontent with the Park regime[5] grew among the rural population, and in the national election of 1969, the approval rate of the ruling Democratic Republican Party of President Park fell by 15 per cent even in the rural areas, which traditionally had been regarded as a favourable voting constituency for President Park.

Saemaul Undong was initiated to ameliorate the widening gap by utilizing resources accumulated with industrial development. In the winter of 1970, the Government received a report on the overproduction of cement and improvised a plan to distribute the excess to rural people. The Government first distributed 355 packs of cement to each of the 34,665 rural communities free of charge with one restriction: usage for the welfare of the entire community. The plan received a favourable public reaction and achieved significant results beyond the Government's prediction. The cost of free cement was W4.1 billion[6] but the estimated monetary value of the projects carried out by the rural community was three times the cost, at W12.2 billion (Park and Lee 1997). Encouraged by the success and incorporating the lessons learned from the previous rural development programmes, President Park elaborated a new rural development programme, naming it Saemaul Undong.

Objectives

When Saemaul Undong was initiated, it did not have an official definition of Saemaul Undong. This did not happen until 1973, when the words closest to a definition could be found in President Park's impromptu comments at the National Convention of the Village Leaders: "We may call this movement as the movement for a better living" (Park 1998, p. 47).

---

[5] Jung-Hee Park led a military coup on May 16, 1961 and became the Chairman of the Supreme Council for National Reconstruction, which incapacitated the Jang Myun administration. He later discharged himself from the army and won the 1963 presidential election as the leader of the newly created Democratic Republican Party. With economic development as a main priority of his administration, he legitimized his rule with strong economic growth and the alleviation of abject poverty, and won the elections in 1967 and 1971. Though the Constitution of 1963 only allowed a person to serve as president for two consecutive terms, Park ran for the presidency a third time in 1971 by amending the constitution and had narrowly winning over Dae-Jung Kim. In October 1972, he declared a state of emergency, dissolved the National Assembly and suspended the Constitution. In December, a new "Yooshin" Constitution was approved, which opened the way for Park to be a lifetime president. Protests calling for the end of Park's dictatorship grew larger among students and later became nationwide. On October 26 1979, Park's regime was ended with his assassination by Jae-Gyu Kim, the director of the National Intelligence Agency.

[6] Approximately $6.8 million (using the exchange rate of $1=W310.58, from http://ecos.bok.or.kr.)

This was later interpreted by Park Jin-whan, special assistant to the President for Saemaul Undong, as a movement to develop the work ethics of farmers by participating in village projects to accelerate rural modernization (Park 1998). Though different interpretations existed regarding how to define the objectives of Saemaul Undong, most agreed that the aim was to generate economic, social and attitudinal improvements. The most broadly accepted objectives are (a) income generation, (b) living environment and basic rural infrastructure improvement, and (c) capacity-building and attitudinal change.

Annual progress

In accordance with the change in the focus and scope of village level projects, Saemaul Undong could be divided into three phases. In the initial phase, the priority at the village level was given to the improvement of the physical infrastructure. A list of exemplary projects was developed by the Government and given to the villages as a guideline to help villagers to develop general ideas on what they could do for themselves. As villagers gained more confidence in their ability and the basic infrastructure necessary to improve agricultural productivity, Saemaul Undong shifted its focus, and income-generation projects were gradually initiated while the scope and size of each living condition improvement project increased. In the last phase, the focus was shifted towards capacity-building and attitudinal changes, while the scope of the projects became broader. Activities in urban areas, factories and corporations became more common, which changed Saemaul Undong into a national campaign. With the demise of President Park in 1979, the new Government decided to privatize Saemaul Undong. In 1980, the non-governmental Central Headquarters for Saemaul Undong was established and with that Saemaul Undong as the Government-led rural development programme ended.

Outputs, outcomes and achievements

Different reviews presented different interpretations on the achievement of Saemaul Undong. On one side, some argued that Saemaul Undong achieved most of its objectives and brought unprecedented success in rural development based on Government statistics which showed that most of the objectives had been achieved.

On the other side, some have claimed that surveys and data, including the impact of Saemaul Undong after 1979, showed a different picture. They argue that, though it was true that Saemaul Undong accomplished the quantifiable objectives directed from the central Government with massive resource mobilization and the enforcement of the authoritarian Government, the impact was not sustained, and was therefore not successful.

This section will show that Saemaul Undong brought about meaningful improvements in the social development dimension: improvements in basic infrastructure; increased accountability of local governments; and the empowerment of villagers, while producing limited impact on income poverty reduction and economic development.

Income generation and income poverty reduction

Various income-generation projects were implemented with the aim of increasing rural household income and reducing poverty. New agricultural technologies and improved crop varieties were introduced and the usage of chemical inputs and fertilizers became more widespread. Improved physical infrastructure helped productivity increase and income grow by opening a new window of opportunity for villagers to venture into new activities and by providing efficient access to the markets, resources and assets necessary for their work. The absolute poverty rate decreased in 1970 and especially in 1978, when the proportion of rural people in total absolute poverty was less than that of urban people (table 1). In terms of income, rural household income recorded a six-fold increase from W255,800 in 1970 to W1,531,300 in 1979, even at one point exceeding that of urban households in 1976 (table 2). Income sources for rural people also became diversified and the portion of non-agricultural income also rose (table 3).

The positive impact of Saemaul Undong on reducing rural poverty and increasing income was, however, limited. The relative poverty rate of rural areas shot up again to 11.2 per cent in 1978 (table 1). What is more important is the pertinaciously low level of agricultural income. From 1963 to 1985, the ratio of per capita agricultural income to per capita urban working income constantly remained below 40 per cent (table 4). In fact, the increase in rural household income in the 1970s was mostly due to the heavy subsidization of rice prices by the Government and a steady increase in off-farm employment opportunities, neither of which were directly linked to Saemaul Undong. Though income-generation projects contributed to agricultural productivity growth and increasing incomes, the causal relation between the two was not as strong and direct as that of the high price policy (Park and Ahn 1999).

The decrease in the number of poor people in rural areas could also be due to the transfer of poverty to urban areas. As the portion of urban population to total population increased from 34 per cent in 1966 to 57 per cent in 1980, the portion of urban people in poverty proportionately rose from 34 per cent in 1965 to 56 per cent in 1978 (Seo 1981). This implied that, despite Saemaul Undong, urban migration continued and subsequently, rural poor people, seeking a high labour wage, migrated to form part of the urban poor.

In conclusion, while Saemaul Undong helped to alleviate absolute poverty in rural villages by providing better access and opportunities, it was not sufficient to address the structural problems of agriculture, which required much more physical and financial investment and drastic changes in agricultural policies rather than the massive mobilization of human labour.

Table 1. Change in the poverty rate and the number of people living in poverty
(Thousands of people, percentage)

	1965			1970			1978		
	Urban	Rural	Total	Urban	Rural	Total	Urban	Rural	Total
Number of people in absolute poverty (thousands)	4 244	7 505	11 749	2 006	5 548	7 554	2 552	1 995	4 547
Distribution of people in absolute poverty (percentage)	36.1	63.9	100.0	26.6	73.4	100.0	56.1	43.9	100.0
Absolute poverty rate	54.9	35.8	40.9	16.2	27.9	23.4	13.75	10.80	12.28
Relative poverty rate (percentage)	17.9	10.0	12.2	7.0	3.4	4.8	16.6	11.2	13.9

Source: Data based on Sang-Mok Seo (1981). "Definition of poverty and time series analysis", accessed from www.kdi.re.kr/kdi/report/report_read05.jsp?pub_no=00003580 on March 21 2008.

Note: In this study, absolute poverty is defined as a monthly household income which is below W20,000 for an urban household and W17,000 for a rural household. Relative poverty is defined as a household income lower than one third of the average national household income level (all incomes are estimated in 1980 Korean won).

Table 2. Ratio of rural household income to urban household income
(Unit: Korean won)

Year	Average monthly income of urban household (A)	Average monthly income of rural household (B)	Ratio (B)/(A) (percentage)
1967	20 720	12 456	60.1
1970	31 770	21 317	67.1
1973	45 850	40 059	87.4
1976	95 980	96 355	100.4
1979	219 133	185 624	84.7

Source: Soon-Won Kwon (1997). "Korean experience in poverty alleviation with special reference to the Saemaul Undong", *Social Security Review*, vol. 13, No. 1, June (Korean Social Security Association), p. 194.

Table 3. Farming household income in the 1970s
(Unit: Korean won)

Year	Household income	Agricultural income		Non-agricultural income	
	Amount	Amount	Ratio (percentage)	Amount	Ratio (percentage)
1970	255 800	194 000	75.9	61 800	24.1
1973	480 700	390 300	81.2	90 400	18.8
1976	1 156 300	921 200	79.7	235 100	20.3
1979	1 531 300	1 531 000	68.7	696 200	31.3

Source: National Council of Saemaul Undong Movement in Korea (1999) "Saemaul Undong in Korea", p. 38, accessed from www.saemaul.com/center/www/caups/down/issue/새마을운동(영문).pdf on 25 March 2008.

Table 4. Comparison of per capita rural income to urban income
(Unit: thousands of Korean won)

Year	Urban household		Rural household		Ratio	
	Per capita income (A)	Per capita working income (B)	Per capita income (C)	Per capita agricultural income (D)	(C/A)	(D/B)
1963	12	60	15	24	1.22	0.40
1965	16	92	18	28	1.09	0.31
1970	55	254	43	67	0.79	0.26
1975	140	538	155	250	1.11	0.43
1980	558	2 144	527	705	0.94	0.33
1985	1 087	3 912	1 220	1 492	1.12	0.38

Source: Lee, Dong-Pil and others (2004). Analysis on Cause and Trend of Rural-Urban Gap in Income and Development Level, Research R490-1 (Seoul, Korea Rural Economics Institute).

Note: The income is calculated in nominal price.

Living environment improvement and basic rural infrastructure establishment

It seems that Saemaul Undong led to substantial improvements in rural infrastructure (table 5). In fact, most studies concur that Saemaul Undong brought significant improvements in the rural living environment and infrastructure. Enlarged and extended roads made mechanized farming possible, while the extension of telephone lines and electrification provided timely information and enabled villagers to cope with changing market situations.

The improvement consequently created a virtuous circle of human development. Improved basic infrastructure helped to increase productivity and income, with better access and wider opportunities, while also creating a healthier environment with better sanitation. Their experience of cooperation with the Government provided learning-by-doing opportunities for building capacities in project management. It also boosted confidence and changed attitudes, which led to the empowerment of people in the villages and transformations in local governance.

Table 5. Major achievements of some Saemaul Undong projects in the 1970s

Project	Unit	Target	Performance	Ratio (percentage)
Village roads expansion	Km	26 266	43 558	166
Farm feeder roads construction	Km	49 167	61 797	126
Small bridge construction	Ea	76 749	79 516	104
Small reservoirs construction	Ea	10 122	10 742	106
Traditional small irrigation (channel)	Ea	22 787	28 352	124
Traditional small irrigation (raceway)	Km	4 043	4 442	109
Traditional small irrigation (embankment)	Km	17 239	9 180	53
Village centre construction	Ea	35 608	37 012	104
Public warehouse construction	Ea	34 665	22 143	64
Housing improvement	Ea	544 000	225 000	42
Village layout renovation	Ea	-	2 747	-
Sewage system upgrade/construction	Km	8 654	15 559	179
Electricity supply system installation	Household	2 834 000	2 777 500	98
Telephone lines		-	345 240	
Saemaul factory construction/operation	Ea	950	717	75
Reforestation	Ha	744 354	347 153	47

Sources: Chang-Soo Choe (2005). "Key Factors to Successful Community Development: The Korean Experience", Discussion Paper No. 39, November, Institute of Developing Economies (Chiba, Japan, JETRO), p. 5, as cited in National Council of Saemaul Undong, "Saemaul Undong in Korea" (1999), p. 24, table 1; and Sung-hwan Ban, "Development of the rural infrastructure and the Saemaul Undong", appendix table 1 in Man-Gap Lee (1981). ed., *Toward a New Community Life,* Seoul National University Institute of Saemaul Undong Studies p. 321, as cited in appendix table 1.

Note: Table is based on data from articles by Sung-hwan Ban and Chang-Soo Choe.

Capacity-building and attitudinal change

The Ministry of Home Affairs' conception of rural villagers was not very different from the stereotypical traditional interpretation of them that outside development agents held at that time. The Ministry's view of farmers was that they were conservative, unwilling to participate in cooperative efforts, hedonistic and lazy. The Ministry ascribed these bad habits and negative attitudes to low agricultural productivity and chronic poverty and argued that rural development was only possible with significant changes in rural people's attitudes. The Ministry attempted to change their pessimistic and fatalistic attitude and promoted modern values focusing on three core values—diligence, cooperation and self-reliance through large-scale training, seminars and workshops.

Saemaul Undong received some favourable responses and achieved some meaningful results in its campaign for attitudinal change. More than 500,000 people took part in Saemaul Undong trainings from 1972 to 1979. Based on a survey of the 150 Saemaul Undong leaders, conducted in 1974, 38 per cent chose increased cooperation spirit among villagers as the most positive result brought about by Saemaul Undong (Park 1974). In another survey, villagers chose changes in behaviour, spirit of cooperation and confidence of a better future as positive changes made possible by Saemaul Undong (Brandt and Lee 1979).

Bad habits and old attitudes, however, were not the main causes of rural economic difficulties. The sluggish agricultural productivity growth and persistent poverty had more to do with the failure of the Government to deliver essential assistance and resources or to provide people with effective measures to cope with deteriorating terms of trade. Some of the spirits and attitude that Saemaul Undong tried to promote, moreover, did not need further encouragement.

The culmination of all those so-called attitudinal changes was in the empowerment of people and improvements in local governance. Saemaul Undong created an enabling environment where rural people voiced their opinions and made themselves heard. Government agencies and officials were considered as potential sources of assistance rather than as feared exploiters. The latter part of this chapter will first examine the meaning of changes in three core values that Saemaul Undong promoted, and will review the attitudinal changes that were inadvertently brought forth but contributed to social development in rural villages.

Diligence

It seemed that designating laziness as one of the main causes of rural poverty was overstretching the logic. Korean farmers, as with other farmers in developing countries, seemed to have lived a very challenging life. Farm wives, for example, had to raise children, make clothes, do the laundry, cook meals, collect firewood, fetch water, work all day in the fields and do some additional side jobs. It was even more absurd to assert that, before 1971, farmers held values that made them lazy, while at the same time workers in the city, who were mostly of farm origin, created the industrial "miracle" (Brandt 1981). If there was a new industriousness linked to the success of Saemaul Undong, it would be caused by the new opportunities and resources created for profitable agriculture rather than by a change in values (Brandt 1981).

Self-reliance

Saemaul Undong contributed to rural farmers becoming self-sufficient and free from shortages of food by being able to produce enough food for themselves, and more confident about their capability. There was, however, a built-in contradiction associated with the goal of self-reliance since the changes brought about by Saemaul Undong required further outside assistance (Brandt 1981). Commercial farming required continuous technological development and adaptation to the market situation. It also had an intrinsic vulnerability to external shocks. Self-reliance became difficult for farmers due to the increased uncertainties that accompanied their shift from subsistence to commercialized agriculture. Dependency on the Government actually increased in many ways, and government officials complained that villages were always asking for help instead of trying to help themselves, while farmers complained of patronizing bureaucratic superiority (Brandt 1981).

Cooperation

Most Asian rural communities, including Korean rural villages, shared the traditional values of cooperation developed throughout a long history of agricultural cultivation. Saemaul Undong linked the traditional sense of cooperation to individual gains and modified the concept to fit into the modernization process. In the beginning, the Government increased "participation" by mobilizing villagers through coercive pressure. Later, as people gradually realized the benefit of village activities, voluntary cooperation started to take place. Over a period of several years, people learned how to work together to develop estimates on the resources required, to get necessary assistance from outside and to motivate some reluctant farmers. This calculated cooperation, however, later became obsolete in the new society built by Saemaul Undong itself. The increase of cash crop farmers and the commercialization of agriculture, which was less dependent on cooperation with one another and more on machines and technologies, undermined the cooperation and solidarity found in the village institutions in the past (Brandt 1981). Individualism steadily penetrated rural society, fostered by the mass media, commercialized agriculture and rampant commercialism (Brandt 1981).

Participation and empowerment of people

As much as it was top-down and centralized, Saemaul Undong was almost equally bottom-up in some ways despite the political and social atmosphere in the Republic of Korea at that time. While the main role of the central Government was limited to leading and coordinating the nationwide activities of the various stakeholders, villagers, at the opposite end, took responsibility for village level activities, tailoring them to the needs and circumstances of the communities.

Saemaul Undong also introduced a new kind of community-based leadership, which was different from that of the traditional village chiefs. While village chiefs had been paid and appointed by the Government from among old villagers, Saemaul Undong leaders were elected by the villagers usually among relatively young people and served the villages without any compensation. They represented the interests of their villages to the local authorities and sometimes did not hesitate to challenge or confront the local officials. Under this new leadership, the villagers worked together for a common goal. The new experience allowed the people to realize their capacity and empowered them vis-à-vis the Government.

The empowerment, however, was a limited experience with regard to development issues and was never further developed or transferred to become fully fledged political activism. Villagers were well aware that they were participating in a campaign initiated and implemented by the Government. Their participation was also strictly limited to the activities relevant to Saemaul Undong. They also knew that, though the local government agents were helping them, the agents could always turn into watchdogs for the Government.

Change in local governance

The Government officials historically regarded rural villagers as subjects of their rule, while villagers tended to perceive the officials as exploiters imposing difficult rules upon them. This mutual discordance created distrust between the two sides, which had been a serious obstacle to the introduction of Government-led campaigns in rural villages. With Saemaul Undong, the traditional role of local governments changed from being an instrument of the central Government to a rural development agent assisting villagers. The local government linked villagers' needs to central Government directives and channelled the voice from the field into Government policy. With the help of Saemaul leaders, it delivered Government services and assistance to rural villages and coordinated various kinds of Government support to avoid any confusion, unnecessary duplication and conflicts. Local government policies accordingly became more representative of their constituents.

Gender and Saemaul Undong

As in many other developing countries, women in the Republic of Korea were not traditionally welcome to engage in social issues. Saemaul Undong opened a small window of opportunity for rural women to officially participate in social activities and engage with the government. Initially, their participation was limited to continue the so-called "women's work"; however, they gradually increased their involvement in village activities. Some of the Saemaul woman leaders proactively initiated and successfully implemented projects which were considered part of men's domain. The tenacious efforts made and the outstanding achievements accomplished by women made the public appreciate their capacity and positively changed the general view of women's role in society.

Though the contribution and achievement of women in Saemaul Undong positively changed the conservative attitude towards women, it did not lead to sustainable awareness of women's rights in society, nor did it create systematic institutional changes inside the Government for the empowerment of women. The encouragement by the Government for the further engagement of women was partly to address the feminization of agriculture and rural villages caused by massive migration of men to urban areas (Cho and Tinker 1981). From the beginning, there was no such strategy developed for gender mainstreaming to address the deep-rooted social bias and discrimination against women. The positive changes were solely brought about by women's own efforts, which were not scaled up into policy or institutional change.

III. FACTORS FOR SUCCESS

Many factors can be attributed to the achievements of Saemaul Undong. While some are context-specific circumstances which created a favourable environment for community-based rural development programmes, others are policies deliberately designed for Saemaul Undong. This chapter first identifies favourable pre-conditions specific to the Korean context, lists policies and strategies developed specifically by the Government for Saemaul Undong, and finally details village-level contributions.

Pre-conditions

Homogeneous communities with strong tradition of cooperation

Rural communities in the Republic of Korea had some distinct features: a long history of settlement by people usually related to each other by kinship; rice farming as their main economic activity; and sharing traditional customs and autonomous norms based on Confucian teaching. Ethnic homogeneity also contributed much towards cohesive cooperation, thus reducing the possibility of disputes and conflicts. Like many other rural villages in Asian countries, rural villagers in the Republic of Korea had, for a long time, already known and realized the benefits of cooperation. Each village also had its own autonomous rules and customs for cooperation called *doorae, gyae* and *hyang-yak. Doorae* is a more than 500-year-old tradition of cooperation to do the difficult work that could not be done by one household. *Gyae* is a small savings scheme especially popular among housewives. The age-old tradition called *hyang-yak* is an autonomous customary norm promoting cooperation and good deeds among villagers, based on its Confucian tradition. This rich social capital in rural villages made rural people feel less hostile towards Saemaul Undong since collaboration for the common good was not a foreign idea. Saemaul Undong in turn further developed the traditional exercise of cooperation to be more deliberate and sophisticated.

Egalitarian society with land reform

It has been noted that large inequalities in assets, such as property and land, and prestige have a tendency to reduce community solidarity, and often make the task of creating viable participatory organizations and projects impossible (Goldsmith 1981). Disproportionate control of assets and resources by a small number of local elites increased the risk of local capture and the domination of benefits of a development programme by the local elites, hindering the possible impact of any community development programme.

Undoubtedly, one of the major reasons for the relative success of Saemaul Undong is the egalitarian rural village structure created after the comprehensive land reform. In 1950, the Government enacted a land reformation law, which prohibited tenant farming and put a ceiling on land ownership of only three hectares of land per person. The land reform practically got rid of major absentee landlords from rural villages, which, coupled with migration to the cities of both rich peasants and landless and near-landless tenants, had the effect of levelling incomes and homogenizing the rural population. In 1970, when Saemaul Undong was initiated, 94 per cent of rural households held farms smaller than two hectares, while 64 per cent held less than one hectare (Goldsmith 1981). With the demise of traditional ruling elites, the social and political structure in the village became more equitable. The relatively egalitarian structure was favourable to Saemaul Undong with villagers in similarly poor situations and few possibilities of local capture.

Solid and continuous economic growth

Many Governments in developing countries often face difficulties in pursuing their development programmes due to budgetary constraints. Needing to overcome the multifaceted challenges of poverty and constrained by limited financial sources, developing countries could not usually commit themselves to long-term development programmes. Having learned the importance of physical assistance after the failure of the previous rural development programme, the Government of the Republic of Korea utilized resources made available by sustained economic growth to support Saemaul Undong. The constant economic growth mitigated the extra burden of expenditure incurred by Saemaul Undong. The ratio of the Government assistance for Saemaul Undong to tax revenue was on average 2.48 per cent and did not go above 5 per cent at any point except in 1975. Strong and continuous economic growth increased tax revenue, which allowed the Government to continuously support and lead the programme with little budgetary concern. Sustained economic growth also helped to increase the market for agricultural products by raising the income of urban industrial workers who were at the same time major consumers of rural products.

Table 6. Annual expenditure of Saemaul Undong, tax revenue and gross domestic product
(Unit: billions of Korean won)

Year	Community Contribution (A)	Government assistance (B)	Others (C)	Total contribution (A)+(B)+(C)	Revenue (D)	Gov't assistance/ revenue (B)/(D)	GDP (E)	Community contribution/ GDP (A)/(E)	Gov't assistance/ GDP (B)/(E)	Total contribution/ GDP
1971	8	4	0	12	1 065	0.39%	3 412	0.24%	0.12%	0.36%
1972	27	4	2	33	1 374	0.26%	4 218	0.65%	0.09%	0.77%
1973	77	17	2	96	1 376	1.24%	5 454	1.41%	0.31%	1.76%
1974	84	31	18	133	1 993	1.55%	7 778	1.08%	0.40%	1.71%
1975	129	165	2	296	3 197	5.17%	10 386	1.24%	1.59%	2.85%
1976	150	165	7	323	4 392	3.76%	14 305	1.05%	1.15%	2.26%
1977	217	181	69	467	4 927	3.67%	18 356	1.18%	0.98%	2.54%
1978	295	233	106	634	6 416	3.63%	24 745	1.19%	0.94%	2.56%
1979	328	227	203	758	8 541	2.66%	31 732	1.03%	0.71%	2.39%
total, ave	1 316	1 027	409	2 751	33 281	2.48%	120 385	1.01%	0.70%	1.91%

Source: Park, J. and D. Ahn (1999). "Saemaul Undong and Yushin Regime", *Critical Review of History*, No. 2, Institute of Korean Historical Studies (Seoul), p. 51.

Note: Tax revenue data is from the statistical website of the National Statistics Bureau and Gross Domestic Production, accessed from www.kosis.kr on 22 February 2008.

National leadership and political commitment

It has been argued that no policies or programmes can be successfully implemented without the commitment of the Government, and Saemaul Undong was no exception. Strong commitment and leadership from the very top played a crucial part in its success. It was President Park, with his strong will and commitment, who initiated, designed and provided continuous support for Saemaul Undong. He made Saemaul Undong a top priority of his Government, checking monthly progress, inviting villagers to cabinet meetings to give presentations, and making surprise visits to villages and training centres. A strong commitment from the top leader enabled effective vertical integration linking all the levels of government and created a holistic approach horizontally mobilizing resources and coordinating plans among the relevant ministries. With Saemaul Undong a top Government priority, Government officials made significant efforts for the programme's success as they knew their personal gains, such as promotion, were dependent on their performance.

Policies and strategies of the Government

Holistic approach

Saemaul Undong took a distinctive holistic approach by combining training in capacity-building and institution-building with physical development activities based on the villagers' needs. The programme started with relatively small projects that could produce distinctive changes in the village but be accomplished relatively easily so that the villagers could realize their capacity and build confidence in themselves. At the same time, it provided training on sharing the practical experiences of Saemaul leaders in successful villages and delivering practical knowledge and technical skills necessary for project management. Villagers could better manage their activities with newly acquired knowledge, which in turn produced better results and strengthened their confidence even further, creating a virtuous circle of development.

Saemaul Undong also comprehensively dealt with various challenges that the villagers identified, coping with the multidimensional challenge of poverty. By not focusing on a specific challenge, it efficiently dealt with the diverse but interlinked adversities that rural villages faced. Under broad Government guidelines, priorities were determined by the people and were carried out step by step.

Horizontal coordination

To effectively address the multidimensionality of poverty and to deliver the comprehensive development plan package in cooperation with rural villagers, the Government of the Republic of Korea devised a distinct approach of horizontal coordination. The Government delegated the authority of coordination to the Ministry of Home Affairs, under which all relevant ministries were mobilized. A committee, chaired by the Minister of Home Affairs, was formed in the central Government and the relevant ministries and organizations discussed and coordinated their plans under the guidance of the Ministry of

Home Affairs. In each level of local government, a special committee for coordination was also created. Comprehensive development plans for each village were managed by the relevant department congruent to their work and channelled up to the relevant ministries in the central Government, effectively covering all the issues concerned.

Vertical integration

Using the centralized and hierarchical administrative system, Saemaul Undong effectively created vertical integration linking villages, local governments and the central Government. Each level of government managed programmes under its control and reported to the higher level authority. The central Government provided general guidelines and directions and coordinated the overall management of the plan. The local government acted as a pipeline conveying the voices from the villages to the top and transferring directions from the top to the village. Local governments were permitted to modify at their own discretion the action plans under their jurisdiction to some extent reflecting local conditions and the opinions of the villagers. Each level of local government was also accountable for monitoring and coordinating the activities of the lower level governments. From the central Government to the villages, government officials and villagers were linked vertically, which made effective communication and cooperation possible.

Incentive system and competition

The selective approach taken by the Government acted as strong motivation for the people to be actively involved. In 1973, based on performance evaluation, the Government disqualified 6,108 villages out of a total of some 30,000 villages from receiving further assistance for the following year. The principle of "more assistance to more successful villages" acted as an effective stimulator, increasing competition among villages and promoting more participation for better achievement (Kim 2000). Later, the Government classified all the rural villages into three categories and selectively provided villages with assistance, favouring those advancing towards a "self-sustainable community" while spurring the lagging villages to catch up with others.

Conversely, the Government also provided successful villages and their leaders with rewards. They were regarded as national heroes and presented their stories at cabinet meetings and training courses and in schools. Local government officials, with their personal interests regularly at stake, sometimes every day, visited rural villages and kept detailed records of village achievements. The strong message from the top was that rural development was a national priority and it was to be implemented through Saemaul Undong, and that they would be held accountable for its success (Goldsmith 1981).

Capacity-building training programmes

Practical and experience-based training was given to more than 500,000 people during the course of Saemaul Undong from 1972 to 1980 (Park 1974). Programmes provided practical skills and technologies on project management and new tools and technologies in agriculture. Practical knowledge gained from training programmes helped to improve their living standards, which in turn led the villagers to change their traditional attitude and strengthen the lessons of attitudinal change provided by other training. Training also provided the participants with a chance to share knowledge and exchange views on their failures and successes while serving as a communication channel relaying the suggestions and opinions of the participants to the government.

Public relations

Mass media from television and radio to newspapers and magazines were widely and extensively utilized for disseminating information on, drawing more attention to, and participation in Saemaul Undong. Under the management of the Ministry of Home Affairs, all three domestic television channels and radio channels frequently broadcasted updated news and success stories. During the Saemaul Undong period, early in the morning each day, all radio channels broadcasted the Saemaul song and special programmes on village news and stories. This massive public relations drive certainly helped to deliver the necessary information to the villagers and to promote broader participation and engagement. The messages, however, were disproportionately dominated by dramatic success stories and mostly served the interest of the Government rather than channelling the voices of the bottom to the top.

Village level efforts

Community participation

For any rural development programme to be successful, active participation and ownership among villagers is a prerequisite. With Saemaul Undong, the tradition of cooperation developed to become calculated participation with the experience of consensus building, and collective decision-making and implementation in managing village projects.[7] According to a report by the Ministry of Home Affairs, between 1971 and 1979, each rural person contributed 12 days of work per year, totalling 1.1 billion work days, to Saemaul Undong. In 1978, a large-scale survey done by the Korea Rural Economic Institute showed that 67 per cent of the respondents said that they attended all the village meetings held in their villages, while another 28 per cent said they attended often (Boyer and Ahn 1991).

A close linkage between personal interests and village projects can be ascribed as the main reason for the active participation. When the programme began, village level participation was mobilized by the local government and was limited to the passive provision of labour. Having observed the positive changes and realized the possible benefits, villagers gradually became more proactive. Under the limited autonomy they had in

---

[7] Cooperation in Saemaul Undong could be said to be more goal-oriented and systemized. The Saemaul council systematically managed cooperation projects, which were evaluated to see whether they achieved their target or not. In this sense, cooperation in the programme was more systematic compared to traditional collaboration among people.

implementing projects, they became actively engaged in village-level decision-making and the implementation process. The selective assistance approach and public relations drive by the Government increased the villagers' interest and the competition among them. Greater assistance to more successful village policies led to a spirit of competition among villages, resulting in the increased participation of villagers.[8] The massive dissemination of success stories via the mass media also attributed to promoting a more competitive spirit, positive attitude and hope for change among the villagers.

The active participation that the Government intended to promote was probably not for promoting grass-roots representative democracy in villages. It was rather a tool to rapidly achieve more outcomes in a short period of time by mobilizing people. Inadvertently, the experience of participation provided villagers with a chance to experience grass-roots democracy and to have increased influence, though with some reservation, on the local governments. This increased influence, however, did not lead to a pro-democracy movement against the regime.

Devotion and commitment of Saemaul leaders

Much research has identified the crucial presence of an organizational or political "entrepreneur" that mobilizes and leads people in collective activities as one of the key factors in successful local development. The democratically selected young male and female leaders of Saemaul Undong played an important role in promoting participation and in eventually introducing democratic leadership to the villages. One common denominator shared by almost all of the success cases was the devotion and dedication of the leaders in the villages. Most villagers pointed to the devoted and diligent Saemaul leaders as the number one factor of success.

It is interesting that, though they were the potentially powerful local leaders often with strong local support, Saemaul leaders never became a challenge to the Government authority. Though it was not clear whether it had predicted a possible threat and had exercised precautionary measures, the Government banned Saemaul leaders from joining any political party. On the other hand, people, who must have been fully aware of the commanding involvement of the Government in Saemaul Undong, would not dare to use the very opportunity provided by the Government to turn against it.

IV. LIMITATIONS AND CRITICISMS

Failure in adaptation

In the late 1970s, after completing most of its planned activities, Saemaul Undong was in need of transformation in order to better help farmers to adjust to the different rural

---

[8] In some case they were elected by the villagers, while in others, the leader was designated according to consensus among villagers. In other cases, some people volunteered to be Saemaul leaders.

environments. However, it failed to make the necessary changes and lost momentum. The spread of individualism and the commercialization of agriculture brought by Saemaul Undong, ironically, reduced the importance of communal cooperation and self-reliance in rural economic activities and daily lives. Further income increases required more material inputs and more advanced technology rather than increased cooperation.

A lack of a decent exit strategy, though, could be easily found in many Government-initiated programmes. Uplifted by their success, the Government often dragged and prolonged the termination of some programmes until they fizzled out. The undefined ending can also be seen as a lesson learned, but is not enough to completely deny it all of its achievements.

Ambiguity in scope

Even before Saemaul Undong, each ministry in the Government had already developed and implemented its own plans directly or indirectly related to rural development, which was later incorporated under the name of Saemaul Undong. It was therefore difficult to clearly distinguish pre-existing programmes from the newly initiated programmes for Saemaul Undong, leaving the possibility of exaggeration of its achievements. Though it was evident that rural development was accelerated by Saemaul Undong, it may be difficult to isolate the activities and programmes of Saemaul Undong and its exact outcome and impact.

The difficulty of clear assessment, however, did not negate the positive changes brought about by Saemaul Undong. The successful mixture and coordinated activity could in some way suggest that the scope of work was comprehensive enough and the horizontal coordination among ministries was adequate and appropriate.

Politically motivated for sustaining dictatorship

The most widely accepted criticism of Saemaul Undong is that it was not a rural development programme but rather a propaganda campaign to mobilize the public for President Park's political gain. Some have claimed that President Park used Saemaul Undong to sustain his illegitimate Fourth Republic[9] and to gain much needed political support from his traditional advocates in rural areas against growing criticism and protests in urban cities. They also argued that, to advertise the changes brought by Saemaul Undong, development efforts were often concentrated on more visible villages close to highways, while remote communities were given less assistance.

---

[9] On 17 October 1972, President Park took a series of drastic measures to give himself life-long presidency. He declared a state of emergency, proclaimed martial law, dissolved the National Assembly and suspended the Constitution. He then promulgated a new Constitution called the "Yooshin (revitalizing) Constitution," launching the Fourth Republic. The change ultimately concentrated all the power of the Government of the Republic of Korea to President Park and deeply damaged the civil liberty and democracy movements.

There seems, however, to be no Government policies, including development policies, that are neutral and free from political influences and interests. Government policies and programmes should be evaluated on the extent to which they benefit the targeted people.

Top-down model under an authoritarian regime

Critics also claim that, since Saemaul Undong was implemented depending solely and heavily on President Park's dictatorial leadership, it would not work in a democratic political context. It is quite true that, without strong leadership and drive, it would have been very difficult to mobilize all the resources in such a short period of time and make various stakeholders cooperate closely. Especially in the first phase, top-down directives and, in some cases, even coercion were used to mobilize resources and induce rural people to participate. It could be said that, in some developing countries with frequent regime changes, it would be difficult to continuously and sustainably support such a policy. It is not impossible, however, to provide sustained support for a programme in a democratic regime. Regardless of the type of regime, moreover, it is not the case that all programmes that receive strong support from the leaders achieve success. Commitment and leadership from the top may be one of the prerequisites for a successful development programme; however, that alone is not a sufficient condition.

Increased burden on rural people

The form of contribution changed from labour donation[10] to cash contributions as the focus was shifted from rural infrastructure development to income generation, which required more financial resources. From 1969 to 1979, the average household income increased some nine fold from W0.22 million ($763) to W2.2 million ($4,545), while during the same period, the average household debt rose 13 times, from W13,000 to W173,000 (KOSIS 2008).

More than 50 per cent of the household debt was, however, taken on as a means of increasing production, which could in turn contribute towards increased productivity and income (Kim 2000). With more physical capital, it may have been inevitable that there would be increased debt for investment and this could be acceptable as long as it led to an increase in income. In 1979, the ratio of debt to income was still approximately 8 per cent, a 2 per cent increase from 1969 (KOSIS 2008). It should be noted that, in 1980, the debt to income ratio drastically increased to 13 per cent and by an amount of W340,000 per capita (KOSIS 2008). It is not clear, however, whether this sudden increase was due to the de facto demise of Saemaul Undong or to other factors.

---

[10] In many participatory rural development projects, including Saemaul Undong, villagers took part in some of the activities by providing their labour. They worked in construction building, for example, schools and bridges.

Marginalization of poor people

Though rural villages in the Republic of Korea were relatively egalitarian, there still existed villages with significant inequality and people living in absolute poverty. Despite some measures taken, Saemaul Undong did not fully incorporate the poorest of the poor. In villages with relatively wide economic disparity, villagers experienced greater difficulty in reaching consensus because their interests tended to be more varied. When funds had to be collected or labour donated, the burden was typically heavier for the poorer villagers, who certainly had less cash and were probably less inclined to give their labour away for free, especially when they relied heavily on wage labour to earn a living. It is worth noting that the landless or nearly landless poor who formed some 15 or 30 per cent of the rural population at that time, depending on how poverty was measured, did not generally receive any significant benefit from Saemaul Undong (Brandt 1981). They had little or no farmland to cultivate and the cost of replacing roofs or wiring their homes for electricity was too heavy a burden for them. There was little change in values or attitudes among people in this group, and they generally did not speak favourably of Saemaul Undong (Brandt 1981).

Addressing the poorest of the poor proved to be quite a challenging task for most development programmes. Though the average income of rural households and the general living standards had increased, there were few, or none, of the proactive measures to prevent the further marginalization or incorporate the needs of the extremely poor in Saemaul Undong. Given the severe disparities and the vast number of people living in absolute poverty in developing countries today, careful attention should be paid and delicate strategies should be formulated before any replication of Saemaul Undong is made.

Continued urban migration

Despite some improvements in rural living conditions and increases in income, Saemaul Undong did not reverse the trend of urban migration. The rural population continued to decrease during and after Saemaul Undong, with rural villages filled with the old and the young (table 7 and figure 1). In the early 1960s, the average urban migration rate was 1.3 persons per every 100 persons, but in late 1970 it rose to 3.7 persons (Park and Ahn 1999). This continuous decrease in the rural population indicated that, despite some positive changes, Saemaul Undong was not extensive enough to address the deep-rooted structural problems of rural villages, which rather required systematic and comprehensive strategies and drastic changes in agricultural policies. People constantly suffered from problems such as deteriorating terms of trade for agricultural products, artificial price distortion of agricultural products partly imposed by the Government, and increasing rural household debts.

On the other hand, others have argued that Saemaul Undong was never meant to replace industrial development or to deflect the subsequent urban migration. Economic development in the Republic of Korea was based on industrialization and policymakers never intended to change that course. The goal was to lessen the negative impact of industrialization and the rural urban gap. Saemaul Undong was designed to prepare the rural population to adapt to urban life and to minimize the impact of their migration by providing rural people with technical training in various fields and employment opportunities in Saemaul factories in rural areas.

Table 7. Population growth rate
(Percentage)

Period	Total	Urban	Rural
1955-1960	2.88	5.51	1.96
1961-1965	2.71	5.96	1.29
1966-1970	1.90	7.16	-1.16
1971-1975	1.98	5.37	-0.81
1976-1980	1.84	4.89	-1.12

Source: Sun-Woong Kim (1980) "Urbanization pattern of Korea and urban population increase component", *Korea Development Review,* Spring, p.151.

Figure 1. Rural population change from 1970 to 1985

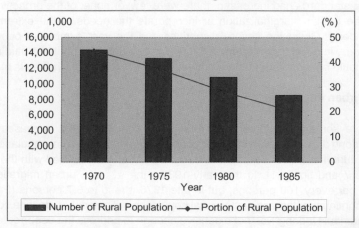

Source: Data from the National Statistics Information Service, accessed from www.kosis.kr on 7 March 2008.

V. LESSONS LEARNED FOR THE TWENTY-FIRST CENTURY

Some have argued that Saemaul Undong, having been implemented some 30 years ago, would not be appropriate in the new millennium. Others have pointed out that the rural development model has evolved with new findings and Saemaul Undong might be outdated. It is true that Saemaul Undong took place a long time ago but also true that we all learn from history and our past experiences.

Though it was an old model, the objectives that Saemaul Undong achieved and the principles on which it was based are not different from the ones that the rural development programmes of today aim to accomplish and on which they are founded. Despite limitations and criticisms, Saemaul Undong promoted social and human development in rural areas. The improvement in rural infrastructure and the living environment reduced the vulnerability of people to natural disasters and disease pandemics and provided easier and broader accesses to and widened opportunities for markets, better education and resources. Saemaul Undong also contributed to reducing absolute poverty and increasing the income level of rural people. In addition, it brought some favourable changes in abolishing archaic customs and empowered women to become development agents. The increased accountability and capacity of local government officials and the empowerment of villagers can also be listed as desirable changes, though most of these were brought about unintentionally.

Those improvements and changes were possible as Saemaul Undong utilized the same policies and strategies that most development agencies emphasize and utilize today for their own rural development programmes. The International Fund for Agricultural Development argued in its *Rural Poverty Report 2001* that the rural poor need legally secure entitlements to assets, especially land and water, technology, access to markets, opportunities to participate in decentralized resource management and access to microfinance (IFAD 2001). It consequently claimed that it is necessary to create a pro-poor policy environment and to allocate significant resources to the poor for the alleviation of poverty and economic growth. The policy recommendation and assessment on the needs and challenges of the rural poor in that report are not so different from the challenges and strategies explained in this paper. In other words, though the terminology was archaic and the methodology and approaches were not clearly defined in the ways that today's development programmes are, what Saemaul Undong achieved and how it did so were not different from the goals that rural development projects and programmes aim to accomplish today.

In fact, the distinction between Saemaul Undong, as well as other successful rural development programmes, and unsuccessful programmes is that the successful programmes developed and implemented workable, practical and specific plans and strategies in accordance with and making use of specific local contexts. Few people dispute or disagree with the importance of the key principles of development, such as building an enabling environment or promoting the inclusive participation of local people in the development programme.

What is more difficult is the substantive development of detailed plans and tools to realize those abstract principles in specific local contexts. What "enabling environment" means and how it can be achieved are totally different from context to context. Saemaul Undong, for example, managed to establish an enabling institutional environment by making use of its administrative structure. Using the centralized structure, it horizontally and vertically linked relevant ministries while it connected the performance of the government officials to the progress of Saemaul Undong, making use of meritocracy at that time. Saemaul Undong also combined favourable social contexts with practical and workable policies and strategies.

In other words, it linked the right policies with the right conditions. It combined a favourable social environment with cleverly designed tools and strategies promoting the involvement of people, while at the same time staying in line with Government policies. Based on strong social capital and an egalitarian rural social structure, the Government promoted the participation of villagers. Continued economic growth supported the programme financially, while strong leadership provided political support.

The most important lessons learned from Saemaul Undong are that it devised appropriate strategies and measures reflecting and making use of specific political, economic and social contexts. Following the model blindly would therefore definitely not achieve the same results in other countries. Developing countries should carefully study their own situation and devise workable and practical solutions of their own. The rest of this chapter will draw key policy suggestions that could be applied in other development programmes and further issues to consider in current development contexts.

Importance of political commitment

Many studies listed the political commitment of the leader or of the Government as one of the key success factors of community development programmes. In fact, many successful community development programmes started with the initiative of top level politicians. Given the fact that community development programmes require long periods of time for planning and implementation, and significant funding, strong and strenuous commitment from the top is a prerequisite for budget allocation and resource mobilization. Political commitment is also important in managing development programmes since government officials tend to put more effort and pay more attention to the policies and programmes that the top leader considers the top priority.

For 10 years, President Park emphasized Saemaul Undong as a top governmental priority. The unwavering commitment of the top leader enabled the Government to allocate 5 per cent of its tax revenue every year to the programme for the 10 years. In this hierarchical and centralized Government system, the commitment from the top leader led high-level Government officials to make significant efforts since their personal interests, such as chances of promotion, depended on the results they delivered to the president. High-level officials encouraged low-level officials by linking their performance evaluation to Saemaul Undong delivery. It would have been difficult to sustain and manage the nationwide programme for a decade without continuous commitment from the top leader.

Creating an enabling environment based on meritocracy and vertical integration

According to Boyer and Ahn (1991), reflecting the focus on democratization and good governance, which are central in the development agenda of today, many countries have adopted or moved towards the decentralization of governance. While centralization has disadvantages, decentralization is not a panacea for ending poverty and underdevelopment in rural areas of developing countries. In many developing countries, the local poor depend heavily on the local elites who dominate resources and power. Abrupt decentralization without a well-laid plan and insightful consideration of the existing power structure may end up legitimately reinforcing the vested interest of the local elite. Decentralization and devolution may not always be better for rural community development programmes in the absence of delicate coordination between the central and the local government and a systematic mechanism to fend off too much influence among local elites and to hear the voices of the poor.

To avoid the local capture of benefits, the government-selected leaders were separate from the traditional village leaders, who usually represented vested interests. Competency-based recruitment of government officials was also important to lessen the influence of the local elites. Local government officials were the people who passed the national civil service examinations and were dispatched from the central Government. Those measures effectively reduced the influence of or domination by the local elites during the course of the Saemaul Undong period.

Delicate coordination between the central and local government reduced overlapping and duplication and resulted in effective management. Using the centralized structure, it horizontally and vertically linked relevant ministries and coordinated their activities and plans. While the central Government set the guidelines and strategies for the whole programme, each level of local government planned and managed its subprogrammes under its jurisdiction. The lower levels of government submitted progress reports and completion reports to the higher levels of government. All the reports were later reviewed by the central Government. Developing countries should devise ways to build the capacity of their governments with careful consideration of their own institutional structure.

Providing motivation and utilizing personal interests

Although the selection of new leaders in the villages and the competency-based recruitment and advancement system were helpful for the programme, this was not enough to ensure the effective implementation of the programme. As with other social programmes, community development programmes are heavily dependent on the devotion and efforts of the people. Saemaul Undong motivated and increased participation by raising the confidence of the village people, aligning their personal interests with the projects and stimulating competition among people.

At the initial stage, the village projects were small and easy to manage, addressing basic needs such as water and sanitation. Observing the benefits and realizing their capacity, the villagers gained self-confidence and belief in the usefulness of the programme. This naturally led to increased participation.

Second, the Government linked the personal interests of the people with the success of the programme. All the village projects were designed to address the basic needs that the villagers said were the most urgent and serious. The implementation of the projects was therefore in their own interest, which reduced possible opposition among the people to the Government decision requiring the usage of their own resources for implementation.

Third, the Government boosted morale and stimulated competition among villagers by selective assistance and information distribution. It provided more assistance for villages with more outputs, and the differences in assistance were publicly announced. Villages with less assistance tried to catch up with those receiving more assistance, increasing overall performance. The dissemination of success stories via nationwide broadcasting also gave hope and raised confidence among people and led to more active participation and higher outputs.

Understanding and incorporating local context

Numerous research studies have noted the importance of local contexts in community development programmes. Saemaul Undong also owed its success to the incorporation of the social, cultural and economic contexts of the Republic of Korea at that time. The notions of diligence and cooperation promoted by Saemaul Undong were based on traditional Korean values. The massive mobilization of resources and strong chain of command from the top level of Government to the villages were made possible due to strong leadership and an authoritarian regime. Strong and continuous economic growth sustained the resources required for rural development while at the same time expanding the market for rural agricultural products. The relatively successful land reforms also created a favourable environment for community-based rural development. These are country- and time-specific conditions that may or may not exist in other developing countries. From the choice of village projects to the capacity-building of local governments, a careful analysis and assessment of specific conditions and contexts should first be conducted to ensure successful rural development. Programmes should be rooted in their own sociocultural contexts at any point in time.

REFERENCES

Ban, Sung-Hwan (1981). "Development of the rural infrastructure and the Saemaul Undong", in Man-gap Lee, ed., *Toward a New Community Life,* Seoul National University, Institute of Saemaul Undong Studies (Seoul), p.321.

Boyer, W. W. and B. Ahn (1991). *Rural Development in South Korea* (Newark, University of Delaware Press).

Brandt, V.S.R. (1981). "Value and attitude change and the Saemaul movement", in Man-gap Lee, ed., *Toward a New Community Life,* Seoul National University, Institute of Saemaul Undong Studies (Seoul).

Brandt, V.S.R. and M. Lee (1979). *Rural Development Movement in Korea*, Korean National Commission for the United Nations Educational, Scientific and Cultural Organization (Seoul).

Cho, H. and I. Tinker (1981). "Women's participation in community development in Korea", in Man-gap Lee, ed., *Toward a New Community Life,* Seoul National University, Institute of Saemaul Undong Studies (Seoul).

Choe, Chang-Soo (2005). "Key factors to successful community development: the Korean experience", Discussion Paper No.39, November, JETRO (Chiba, Institute of Developing Economies).

International Fund for Agricultural Development (IFAD) (2001). *Rural Poverty Report* (New York, Oxford University Press).

Goldsmith, A. (1981). "Popular participation and rural leadership in the Saemaul Undong", in Man-gap Lee, ed., *Toward a New Community Life,* Seoul National University, Institute of Saemaul Undong Studies (Seoul).

Kim, H. (2000). "A critical study on Saemaul Undong (New Community Movement) as a modernization project: focused on the 1970s", *Journal of Korea Rural Development,* vol. 12, No. 2, pp. 21-38.

Kwon, Soon-Won (1997). "Korean experience in poverty alleviation with special reference to the Saemaul Undong", *Social Security Review,* vol. 13, No. 1, June (Korean Social Security Association), p. 194.

Lee, Dong-Pil and others (2004). *Analysis on Cause and Trend of Rural-Urban Gap in Income and Development Level*, Research R490-1 (Seoul, Korea Rural Economics Institute).

National Council of Saemaul Undong Movement in Korea (1999). "Saemaul Undong in Korea", pp. 23 and 38, accessed from www.saemaul.com/center/www/caups/down/issue/새마을운동(영문).pdf on 25 March 2008.

National Statistics Information Services (KOSIS), data accessed from www.kosis.kr on 7 March 2008.

Park, D. (1974). "Faculty articles: role, election and skill of the Saemaul (New Community) Leader", Institute for Public Administration Studies at Graduate School of Public Administration, Seoul National University, vol. 12, No. 2, pp. 2048 –2082.

Park, Jin-Whan (1998). *The Saemaul Movement* (Seoul, Korea Rural Development Institute).

Park, J. and D. Ahn (1999). "Saemaul Undong and Yushin Regime", *Critical Review of History,* No. 2, pp. 37-80 (Seoul, The Institute for Korean Historical Studies), pp. 37-80, accessed from www.riss4u.net/link?id=A30018881.

Park, S. and H. Lee (1997). "State and farmers in modern Korea: an analysis of new village movement", *Korean Political Science Review*, vol. 3, No. 3 (Seoul, Korean Political Science Association).

Seo, S. (1981). *Definition of Poverty and Time Series Analysis on Poverty Population.* (Seoul, Korea Development Institute), accessed from www.kdi.re.kr/kdi/report/report_read05.jsp?pub_no=00003580.

Sung, Myung-jae (2008). "Analysis on the impact of fiscal policy on income distribution structure and poverty rate", *Monthly Public Finance Forum,* No. 148, Korea Institute of Public Finance, October, pp. 8-28.

Sun-Woong Kim (1980). "Urbanization pattern of Korea and urban population increase component", *Korea Development Review,* Spring, p.151.

World Bank (2000). World Development Report 2000/2001 (Washington, D.C., World Bank).

OFF-FARM EMPLOYMENT PARTICIPATION AMONG PADDY FARMERS IN THE MUDA AGRICULTURAL DEVELOPMENT AUTHORITY AND KEMASIN SEMERAK GRANARY AREAS OF MALAYSIA

Norsida Man and Sami Ismaila Sadiya*

Poverty is one of the most serious challenges confronting paddy farmers worldwide, including those in Malaysia. Off-farm employment is an alternative strategy and has the potential to improve the income and well-being of the paddy farmers. This study assesses the off-farm employment decision among 500 paddy farmers in the Muda Agricultural Development Authority and Kemasin Semerak granary areas. Specifically, the study determines the relationship between the determinants of off-farm employment and the off-farm participation decision using descriptive analysis and logit regression methods. The results reveal that the farmers' age, gender and number of dependants, as well as other income and the type of farm were the variables that influenced their likelihood to engage in off-farm employment. Evidently, the variables of farm size and level of education were insignificant in affecting off-farm participation.

I. INTRODUCTION

The term "paddy" refers to rice cultivated in low land with irrigation. Rice farming in Malaysia can be regarded as one of the first irrigated rice production systems observed in Asia. Paddy is produced mainly by small holders with an average farm size of 1.06 hectares (ha) (Malaysia 1976). There are approximately 296,000 paddy farmers in Malaysia, of which 116,000 are full-time farmers who depend on paddy cultivation for their livelihood. Of the paddy farmers, 65 per cent have farms of less than one hectare, while only 4 per cent have more than three hectares. According to the Malaysian Agricultural Research and Development Institute, the total planted area is about 670,000 ha: 386,000 ha within the eight granary areas, about 218,000 ha outside the granary areas and about 70,000 ha representing upland/hill paddy, especially in Sabah and Sarawak, East Malaysia. Average yield for the country is about 3.5 tons per hectare (t/ha)—an average of 4.2 t/ha in the granary areas and 3.2 t/ha elsewhere.

* Norsida Man is a Senior Lecturer at the Department of Agribusiness and Information System, Faculty of Agriculture, Universiti Putra Malaysia, 43400 Serdang, Selangor, Malaysia. Sami Ismaila Sadiya is a graduate student at the School of Graduate Studies, Universiti Putra Malaysia, 43400 Serdang, Selangor, Malaysia. The authors would like to express their gratitude to the Ministry of Science, Technology and Innovation, Malaysia for its support through Science Fund Grant 04-01-04-SF0313, as well as to the Universiti Putra Malaysia.

Malaysia is an inefficient producer of rice—an observation recorded as early as 1988 in a World Bank study. The study noted that the producers' price was double than that of imported rice. It was estimated that 74 per cent of paddy producers' monthly income came from income support measures. This suggests that the Malaysian paddy subsector is non-viable and non-sustainable. Government support for research and development, production and marketing have taken many forms. Credit facilities, fertilizer subsidies, irrigation investment, guaranteed minimum price, income support programmes, subsidized retail price as well as research and extension support (training and advisory), to the tune of billions of dollars for the past 50 years, have been a fiscal drain on the nation. Despite the massive fiscal outlays for this constituency, rice production is still chronically inefficient with respect to meeting the market and population demand. Given the continued decline in cultivated area, negligible gains in productivity, continued increases in the cost of production and decreasing profitability, rice production in Malaysia can be said to be a sunset industry (Pio Lopez 2007).

Rice cultivation in Malaysia is closely associated with the rural population and traditional farmers. Labour in this subsector is characterized by aging farmers and low levels of education. Poverty and dependency is significant in this subsector, and most farmers would be living below the absolute poverty line without Government support. All these considerations lead to sub-optimal allocation of resources at the national level. The situation is further aggravated by the high cost of material inputs—investment in paddy cultivation is not attractive when the open-market price of paddy is considered. Although the government invests heavily in the rice sector for economic reasons, at the farm level, the profit margins have sharply declined. Labour, farm power, fertilizer and agro-chemicals demand about 90 per cent of the total yield. The share of the labour component alone is about 45 per cent (Jayawardane 1996).

The Third Malaysia Plan (1976) reported that the incidence of poverty was as high as 88 per cent among the rice farmers. This was due to the small size of holdings, the prevalence of tenancy, the lack of drainage and irrigation facilities and low yields. Rice production in some parts of Malaysia is facing a host of physical and operational constraints, such as a shortage of land and water resources, escalating prices of agricultural inputs and labour shortages, as well as inefficient water use, low adoption of technology, uneconomic land holdings, high post-harvesting losses and inadequate infrastructure facilities (Morooka, Ohnishi and Yasunobu 1991). A literature review shows that the agricultural sector has a very limited capacity to absorb the existing supply of rural labour and has failed to satisfy even the minimum subsistence requirements of a large proportion of the rural population (Jayasuriya and Shand 1985).

Given the prevalence of surplus labour in rural areas due to mechanization and the high scarcity of land, improving off-farm employment opportunities will be an important way to increase rural household incomes, particularly in the granary areas. Specifically, if farmers are engaged in rural-based non-farm activities (such as manufacturing and trading), they are likely to intensify production efforts and increase agricultural productivity to provide the resources necessary for investment in the rural-based non-agricultural activities. Off-farm employment is generally thought to have a negative impact on the income of the farmers at the household level. However, since there is surplus labour (or farming is not able to absorb the idle family labour), off-farm employment may not compete with farming activities. In order to have a better understanding of this relationship, there is a need to examine the off-farm employment participation among paddy farmers.

Off-farm activities, defined as the participation of individuals in remunerative work away from a "home plot" of land, have been seen to play an increasingly important role in sustainable development and poverty reduction, especially in rural areas (FAO 1998). The economy of off-farm employment has become of interest to governments, non-governmental organizations, international agencies and development practitioners, as such employment has become increasingly common in many developing countries. It has been considered as an alternative income source for the agricultural sector and as an essential way to increase overall rural economic activity and employment in many developing countries.

As economic development progresses, the traditional image of a farm household has shifted to include diverse activities other than agriculture. Many evidences show that the share of rural-household income earned from non-farm activities has been growing substantially. Previous studies found that non-farm income in rural areas accounted for 40 per cent, on average, of total incomes in Latin American countries (Reardon, Stamoulis and Winters 2002). A similar trend was also observed in sub-Saharan Africa, where non-farm income contributed from 30 to 42 per cent of total household income. In Asian countries however, the shares were lower but still significant—around 29 to 32 per cent (Davis 2003). These considerable shares of non-farm income were mainly influenced by the expansion of off-farm employment in rural areas. Many studies found that the majority of farm households were engaged in off-farm employment.

Off-farm activities had also helped to reduce the income uncertainty in rural areas. Diversification of employment helps to smooth income by spreading risk across several activities (Gordon 1999). By reducing the income uncertainty, farm households have opportunities to invest in more advanced agricultural technologies. The adoption of better technology is expected to be highly profitable and will encourage the transition from traditional to modern agriculture. Off-farm employment is crucial to the rural poor, off-farm activities not only provide a significant share of the total income of rural households, but also increase the proportion of the rural poor in the labour force. Participating in off-farm activities offers a diversification strategy for the household, and off-farm incomes provide a source of liquidity in areas where credit is constrained.

It has been widely recognized that off-farm work plays a very important role in augmenting small farmers' income in developing countries. For example, in paddy households in Malaysia in 1979, off-farm income contributed more than three times the annual net income from paddy (Taylor 1981). Therefore, promoting off-farm employment is proposed as a strategy for supplementing the income of farmers.

Corner (1981), referring to the Muda Agricultural Development Authority (MADA) area, observed that there is a need for the expansion of off-farm employment as an anti-poverty strategy, because it will be difficult to raise the farm income of the majority of small paddy farmers above the current poverty level without substantial—and probably inefficient—government subsidies. Furthermore, it is unlikely that the gap between the income levels of the small farms and those of the larger farms and in the non-farm sector can be bridged by a purely agricultural strategy. Shand and Chew (1983) conducted their research in Kelantan, Malaysia and illustrated the significance of off-farm employment of farm households. A large majority of Kemubu farmers had relied heavily on off-farm employment to supplement their farm income in order to achieve even a modest standard of living.

Shand (1986) conducted a study at the Kemubu Agricultural Development Authority area to examine the important factors affecting farm and off-farm allocation of labour. It was found that, due to mechanization, the household labour force was being underutilized in paddy farming and that surplus labour could be tapped by creating more employment through the intensification of farm and off-farm work. Radam and Latiff (1995) conducted research in the Northwest Selangor Integrated Agriculture Development Project area to examine the off-farm labour decision of farmers. They found that the factors influencing the farmers' decision to seek off-farm employment, such as human capital, variables of ages and education levels have the highest impact on off-farm labour participation.

The objectives of the present study are to assess the off-farm employment decisions of 500 paddy farmers in the granary areas of MADA and Kemasin Semerak. Specifically, the study (a) determines the relationship between the determinants of off-farm employment and the off-farm participation decision, (b) describes the characteristics of respondents and their status in off-farm employment, (c) examines the income level of the farm households attributable to paddy farming and off-farm employment, and (d) describes the effect off-farm employment has on paddy farmers.

II. METHODOLOGY

Surveys were conducted between June and July 2007 to examine off-farm employment decision-making among paddy farmers in the granary areas of MADA and Kemasin Semerak. A total of 500 paddy farmers were selected for this study using stratified random sampling. The questionnaire consisted of two types of structured questions: dichotomous choice and multiple categories. The collected data were analysed using Statistical Package for Social Science software for the descriptive analysis and logit regression.

Descriptive analysis was used to describe the characteristics of the variables in terms of the frequencies and the percentage of distribution of the survey, which aided in making comparisons among the variables. The logit model was used to estimate the decision rule for farmers' off-farm work participation; a binary choice model based on the method of maximum likelihood is specified. Each observation was treated as a single draw from a

Bernoulli distribution (Greene 2000). The dependent variable is set up as a 0 and 1 dummy, taking the value 1 for the farm household members who participate in off-farm work and 0 for the members who do not. The predicted value of the dependent variable can be interpreted as the probability of participating in off-farm work, given the values of the independent variables.

A logit model for estimating off-farm work participation may be written as:

$$Y_i^* = \beta X_i + u_i, \; u_i \sim N[0, 1], \; i=1,...,n$$

$$Y_i = \{ \; 1 \text{ if } Y_i^* > 0$$

0 otherwise,

where Y_i is a binary choice which equals 1 if farm household members work off-farm, 0 otherwise; u_i is a continuously distributed variable independent of X_i and the distribution of u_i is symmetric about 0 (Wooldridge 2002). The observed variable Y_i is related to a latent variable Y_i^* (also known as the utility index) that is determined by a matrix of explanatory variables and is the parameter vector to be estimated.

The dependent variable: on and off-farm participation

Since it analyses individual participation in off-farm work, this study uses a dummy variable, which indicates two possibilities of individual participation: off-farm and farm work.

Off-farm work participation is defined in this study as the participation of individuals, whether they own their land or work for a wage, in a secondary or additional job away from his or her own plot of land. Such employment includes (a) primary activities in the non-agricultural sector, and (b) secondary activities in either the agricultural sector (for example, a secondary job at a fish farm, either self-owned or for wages) or the non-agricultural sector (for example, a secondary job in transportation or at a retailer, or a farm household member who owns a barber shop or works as a vendor).

On-farm work participation is defined in this study as the participation of individuals in the agricultural sector as their only job, with no secondary or additional job.

Independent variables: determinants of off-farm participation

Based on empirical studies, the independent variables in this study are the determinants of off-farm work participation. Three groups of independent variables are analysed in this study, as described below.

Individual characteristics

Gender. This dummy variable represents the gender segregation between men and women among household members. The estimated sign of this variable is expected to be negative, which will indicate that women are less likely to participate in off-farm work.

Age. This is used to capture the life-cycle effect on participation in off-farm work. The variable predicted parameter is expected to have a negative sign to indicate that after a certain age the tendency to participate in off-farm work will decline.

Level of education. This represents human capital endowment. It is expected that an increase in individual years of schooling will increase the tendency to engage in off-farm work.

Family characteristics

Number of dependants. This is the number of individuals living in a household. Having more people living in a household indicates a greater burden on the actively working individuals, which is expected to increase the likelihood of participation in off-farm work.

Other income. This is defined as all other non-labour income, including pensions, insurance benefits, transfers, remittances, bonuses and other. Individuals with higher non-labour revenue are expected to be less likely to participate in off-farm work.

Farm characteristics

Farm size. This is the size of any farmland owned by the household, in hectares. Besides capital, this variable indicates land ownership, which reflects asset holding related to poverty. It is assumed that a small farm size is related to a poor farm household and vice versa. Thus, it is expected that off-farm participation is less likely to be favoured by individuals owning larger farms.

Land market. This is related to landless households that rented land or had shared crops. Individuals who come from these types of household tend to have a stronger motivation to engage in off-farm work, given the low level of income generated from farm wages.

III. RESULTS AND DISCUSSION

The empirical results and discussions are presented in the following two subsections. In the first subsection, the descriptive analysis is used to describe the basic features of the data in this study. It describes the respondents' profile and their perceptions of off-farm employment. Meanwhile, the second subsection looks into the logit analysis to study the factors that influence paddy farmers in off-farm employment participation.

Results of the descriptive analysis

Table 1 presents the socio-economic profile of respondents. Three (0.6 per cent) of the respondents were younger than 25 years of age; 173 (35.6 per cent) were between 25 and 50; 307 (61.4 per cent) were between the ages of 51 and 75; and 12 respondents (2.4 per cent) were 76 or older. It is evident that the majority of respondents are between 51 and 75 years of age.

Table 1. Descriptive analysis of respondents

Characteristic	Number	Percentage	Characteristic	Number	Percentage
Age (year)			**Paddy income (RM)**		
<25	3	0.6	<3 000	250	50.0
25-50	173	35.6	3 000-6 000	133	26.6
51-75	307	61.4	>6 000	117	23.4
>75	12	2.4			
Gender			**Off-farm participation**		
Male	406	81.2	Yes	252	50.4
Female	94	18.8	No	248	49.6
Level of education			**Off-farm income (RM)**		
No education	80	16.0	<2 000	111	44.0
Primary education	172	34.4	2 000-3 000	70	27.8
Secondary education	184	36.8	>3 000	71	28.2
Tertiary education	64	12.8			
Farm size			**Total income (RM)**		
0.1-0.8 ha	406	81.2	<4 000	141	28.2
0.9-2.2 ha	78	15.6	4 000-6 000	119	23.8
2.3-3.43 ha	16	3.2	>6 000	240	48.0
Number of dependants			**Change in income after off-farm work**		
< 3	133	26.6	Increase	212	84.1
3-6	285	57.0	Same	37	14.7
> 6	82	16.4	Decrease	3	1.2

Notes: The categories of off-farm participation, off-farm income and change in income after off-farm work consider only those who participate in off-farm employment (252 out of 500 respondents). The surveys were conducted between June and July 2007.

Of the total respondents in both land areas, 406 (81.2 per cent) were male and 94 (18.8 per cent) female. This suggests that paddy farming is dominated by male farmers within the granary areas under study. Of the respondents, 16 per cent had no formal education, 34.4 per cent had primary education, 36.8 per cent possessed secondary education and 12.8 per cent possessed tertiary education. A total of 406 respondents (81.2 per cent) cultivated a small farm and 78 (15.6 per cent) cultivated a medium-sized farm. Only 16 (3.2 per cent) of the respondents cultivated a large farm.

A total of 133 respondents (26.6 per cent) had fewer than three people as dependants; 285 (57 per cent) had between three and six people as dependants, and 82 (16.4 per cent) had more than six dependants. Most respondents had three to six dependants. The total number of respondents that participated in off-farm employment was 252 (50.4 per cent); 248 (49.6 per cent) did not engage in any kind of off-farm employment.

The total number of respondents in the low paddy income category was 250 (50 per cent), while 133 (26.6 per cent) had a mid-level income and 117 (23.4 per cent) had a high income from their paddy yield. A total of 252 respondents reported off-farm income; of those, 111 (44 per cent) had low off-farm income, 70 (27.8 per cent) had a mid-level off-farm income, and 71 (28.2 per cent) had a high income from off-farm employment. The total number of respondents with low total income was 141 (28.2 per cent); 119 respondents (23.8 per cent) had a mid-level total income, and 240 (48 per cent) reported a high total income.

The total number of respondents who experienced an increase in income after engaging in off-farm employment was 212 (84.1 per cent); 37 respondents (14.7 per cent) reported that their income had remained the same, and only three respondents (1.2 per cent) reported having experienced a decrease in income. The decrease in income as experienced by a few farmers was attributed to the high transportation cost to and from the off-farm area. The findings thus suggest that jobs should be made available within a reasonable distance of a farmer's settlement.

It can be concluded that off-farm employment had a positive effect, as well as the potential to decrease poverty among paddy farmers, given that the majority of respondents who engaged in such employment experienced an increase in income.

Logit analysis

A logistic regression model was used to predict the probability factors that determined off-farm participation among the paddy farmers. As indicated above, the dependent variable was off-farm employment participation. Those who were participating were assigned the value of one, while a zero value was assigned if the respondent was not participating. See table 2 for detailed definitions of the variables.

Table 2. Variables and their definition

Variable	Definition
AGECAT1	Respondents who are less than 25 years old
AGECAT2	Respondents who are 25-50 years old
AGECAT3	Respondents who are 51-75 years old
AGECAT4	Respondents who are 76 years or older
EDUCAT1	Respondents who have no formal education
EDUCAT2	Respondents who have primary education
EDUCAT3	Respondents who have secondary education
EDUCAT4	Respondents who have tertiary education
GENDER	Gender
DEPCAT1	Respondents who have less than three dependants
DEPCAT2	Respondents who have three to six dependants
DEPCAT3	Respondents who have more than six dependants
TOICAT1	Respondents who earn less than RM1,000 as other income
TOICAT2	Respondents who earn between RM1,000 and RM2,000 from other income
TOICAT3	Respondents who earn more than RM2,000 from other income
FSCAT1	Respondents who own 0.5-1.0 ha of land
FSCAT2	Respondents who own 1.1-2.0 ha of land
FSCAT3	Respondents who own 2.1-3.0 ha of land
FTCAT1	Respondents who own their own farm
FTCAT2	Respondents who rent the farm
FTCAT3	Respondents who own a farm and rent another

As noted, the independent variables included (a) individual characteristics, such as age, level of education and gender, (b) family characteristics, such as the number of dependants and other income, and (c) farm characteristics, covering farm size, farm type and land holding.

Based on the estimated model, five variables (AGECAT1, GENDER, DEPCAT (1, 2 and 3), TOICAT1 and FTCAT1) were found to be significantly related to the dependent variable (to determine the choice between off-farm employment participation or otherwise).

The interpretation of the negative coefficient of age was that an individual's participation declines as his or her age increases. In other words, the probability of off-farm work participation increases at younger ages, but it will decrease as individuals get older. As shown in table 3, only AGECAT1 (age category of under 25) was significant, with a 0.240 expected likelihood of participating in off-farm employment.

Table 3. The logit results

VARIABLE	B	S.E	WALD	SIG.	EXP(B)
AGECAT1	-1.426	0.444	10.318	0.001*	0.240
AGECAT2	-0.562	0.327	2.979	0.084	0.569
EDUCAT1	0.311	0.441	0.495	0.482	1.364
EDUCAT2	0.366	0.388	0.893	0.345	1.443
EDUCAT3	0.306	0.406	0.568	0.451	0.736
GENDER	- 0.775	0.318	5.955	0.015*	2.172
DEPCAT1	4.179	1.720	5.903	0.015*	0.015
DEPCAT2	4.735	1.709	7.680	0.006*	0.009
DEPCAT3	5.587	1.732	10.409	0.001*	0.004
TOICAT1	-0.602	0.271	4.943	0.026*	0.548
TOICAT2	-0.891	0.756	1.391	0.238	0.410
TOICAT3	-20.043	11908.268	0.000	0.999	0.000
FSCAT1	-21.295	40192.817	0.000	1.000	2E+009
FSCAT2	-22.774	40192.817	0.000	1.000	8E+009
FSCAT3	-23.137	40192.817	0.000	1.000	1E+010
FTCAT1	5.164	1.146	20.289	0.000*	174.832
FTCAT2	2.011	1.199	2.814	0.093	7.474
CONSTANT	-21.302	40192.817	0.000	1.000	0.000

Notes: -2log likelihood=432.943. Percentage of correct prediction=79.4. See table 2 for definition of variables.   *Significant at 5 per cent.

The positive coefficient of education indicates that individuals who had more years of schooling had a higher probability of participating in off-farm work. One additional year of formal education increased the likelihood of individuals to participate in off-farm employment. But looking at table 3, the education variable did not prove to be significant with regard to off-farm employment in either of the granary areas. This suggests that the farmers' participation in off-farm employment was not significantly influenced by their education level. Gender was shown to have a significant effect on off-farm employment. With the addition of a male to a household in the sample size considered, the odds of participating in off-farm employment (versus not participating) increased by a factor of 2.172.

The number of dependants variable also demonstrated a significant correlation with off-farm employment. The positive coefficient indicates that as the total number of dependants increases, the farmer is more likely to participate in off-farm employment to supplement income. DEPCAT1 (the category of farmers who have fewer than three dependants) was significant, with 0.015 expected likelihood of participation as the number of dependants increased. DEPCAT2 (category of respondents who have three to six dependants) was significant with 0.009 expected likelihood of participation, and DEPCAT3 (category of respondents who had above six dependants) also was shown to be significant, with 0.004 expected likelihood of participation.

The negative coefficient of TOICAT (total other income) indicated that as other income, such as pension remittance and gifts from children, increases, there will be less likelihood of participation in off-farm employment. In this case, TOICAT1 was significant with 0.548 likelihood of participation in off-farm employment.

The negative coefficient of FSCAT (farm size) implied that as the size of the farm increased, there was less likelihood of the respondents participating in off-farm employment. But turning once again to table 3, in this case farm size was shown to be insignificant to participation in off-farm employment. FTCAT1 (farm type, category 1) was significant to off-farm employment with 174.832 likelihood of participation.

IV. CONCLUSION AND SUGGESTIONS

Poverty is one of the most serious problems facing paddy farmers in Malaysia. Off-farm employment is an alternative strategy and has the potential to improve the income and well-being of paddy farmers. It also helps to reduce income uncertainty in rural areas. The diversification of employment helps to smooth income by spreading risk across several activities. By reducing income uncertainty, farm households have opportunities to invest in more advanced agricultural technology. The adoption of better technology is expected to be highly profitable and encourages the transition from traditional to modern agriculture.

The present study assessed the off-farm employment decisions of the paddy farmers in the MADA and Kemasin Semerak granary areas. From the study, it can be seen that the paddy farmers have a positive perception of off-farm employment. After receiving the benefits of generating income without negative effect to their farms, those who participated agreed that off-farm employment had improved their standard of living. Those who had not yet participated in such employment were hoping to do so in the future if job opportunities became available. The test of hypotheses of the relationships showed that both individual and family characteristics had a significant effect on off-farm employment, while farm characteristics were insignificant. It can also be deduced that combining both on-farm and off-farm activities would generate more income for households, as compared to relying solely on farm income.

The trend towards bimodal farm-size distribution will likely continue in the granary areas, since it is the middle-aged cohort of farmers who are most likely to work off the farm. Meanwhile, the oldest cohort will not engage in off-farm employment. In order to increase the income level of farmers, measures that boost productivity, such as farm mechanization, improved technologies, increased capital intensities and subsidies, are often advocated. These measures may increase output and revenue in the short run, but farmers will be worse off in the long run. This is because the limited land holding and other resources of farmers prevent the efficient use of much technology. In addition, production techniques are increasingly labour saving, and economies of size give larger operating units an advantage over smaller operations. Therefore, there is a need for the government to formulate policy to increase the availability of off-farm jobs in the vicinity of farmers. Furthermore, the private sector should be encouraged to create income-generating activities in the rural areas.

Training programmes should be directed towards training farmers in skills that can be used in off-farm jobs. There is no specific emphasis on off-farm employment either in the national agriculture or rural development policies of Malaysia. One should be developed as soon as possible, so that the country can reap the benefits of off-farm employment.

REFERENCES

Corner, L. (1981). "The impact of rural outmigration: labor supply and cultivation techniques in a double cropped padi area, West Malaysia", PhD thesis, Macquarie University, Sydney.

Davis, J.R. (2003). "The rural non-farm economy, livelihoods and their diversification: issues and options" (Chatham, Natural Resources Institute).

Food and Agriculture Organization of the United Nations (FAO) (1998). "Rural non-farm income in developing countries", in *The State of Food and Agriculture* (Rome, FAO).

Gordon, A. (1999). *Non-Farm Rural Livelihoods* (Chatham, Natural Resources Institute).

Greene, W.H. (2000). *Econometric Analysis* (New Jersey, Prentice-Hall International, Inc.).

Gregore, P.L (2007). *Economic Reforms for Paddy Sub-sector* (Malaysian Institute of Economic Research).

Jayasuriya. S.K. and R.T. Shand (1985). "Technical change and labor absorption in Asian agriculture: some recent trends", *World Development*, vol.14, No. 3, pp. 415-428.

Jayawardane, S.N. (1996). "Socio-economic constraints and future prospects for crop diversification in minor irrigation schemes", workshop on crop diversification, Colombo.

Malaysia (1976). *Third Malaysia Plan 1976-1980* (Kuala Lumpur, Government Printers).

Morooka, Y., A. Ohnishi and K. Yasunobu (1991). "Reciprocal form of family farm and group farming: a perspective of 'kelompok tani' in Malaysia and Indonesia", *Japanese Journal of Farm Management*, vol. 29, No. 3, pp.13-29.

Pio Lopez, G. (2007). "Economic reforms for paddy sub-sector", *The Star Online*, 25 June, available at http://biz.thestar.com.my/news/story.asp?file=/2007/6/25/business/18087959&sec=business.

Reardon, T.K., G. Stamoulis and P. Winters (2002). *Promoting Farm/Non-farm Linkages for Rural Development: Case Studies from Africa and Latin America.* (Rome, Food and Agriculture Organization of the United Nations).

Radam, A. and Ismail Abd. Latiff (1995). "Off farm labour decisions by farmers in Northwest Selangor Integrated Agricultural Development Project (IADP) in Malaysia", *Bangladesh Journal of Agricultural Economics*, vol. 18, No. 2, pp. 51-61.

Shand, R.T. and T.A. Chew (1983). "Off farm employment in the Kemubu Project in Kelantan, Malaysia".

Shand, R.T. (1986). "Agricultural development, non-farm employment and rural income distribution: a case study in Kelantan Malaysia", in Choe, Y.B. and F.C. Lo, eds. *Rural Industrialization and Non-farm Activities of Asian Farmers, Proceedings of the International Seminar on the Role of Rural Industries for National Development in the Asian Region*, 22-25 April 1985, Seoul, Korea (Rural Economics Institute, Seoul).

Taylor, D.C. (1981). *The Economics of Malaysian Paddy Production and Irrigation* (Bangkok, The Agricultural Development Council).

Wooldridge, J.M. (2002). *Econometric Analysis of Cross Section and Panel Data.* (Massachusetts, The MIT Press).

SUBSCRIPTION FORM

(Please type of print)

NAME: _____

POSITION: _____

ORGANIZATION: _____

ADDRESS: _____

_____

_____

_____

COUNTRY:_____ POSTCODE:_____

TELEPHONE: _____ FACSIMILE: _____ E-MAIL:_____

SUBSCRIPTION RATES FOR ASIA-PACIFIC DEVELOPMENT JOURNAL (2 ISSUES PER YEAR)

❑   1 year   US$ 66.00

❑   3 years   US$ 198.00

Please mail this form together with your subscription fee in US dollars in the form of a bank draft/cheque drawn in a bank in the United States, issued in the name of UN-ESCAP, crossed and marked "Account Payee Only". The draft/cheque may be mailed to the following address:

Chief, Conference Management Unit
Administrative Services Division
Economic and Social Commission for Asia and the Pacific (ESCAP)
United Nations Building, Rajadamnern Nok Avenue
Bangkok 10200, Thailand

✂ --

This publication may be obtained from bookstores and distributors throughout the world.
Please consult your bookstore or write to any of the following:

Sales Section   Tel: (212) 963-8302
Room DC2-0853   Fax: (212) 963-4116
United Nations Secretariat   Telex: 422311 UN UI
New York, NY 10017
United States of America

Sales Section   Tel: (41) (22) 917-1234
United Nations Office at Geneva   Fax: (41) (22) 917-0123
Palais des Nations   Telex : 23711 ONU CH
CH – 1211 Geneva 10
Switzerland

Chief, Conference Management Unit
Administrative Services Division
Economic and Social Commission for Asia and the Pacific (ESCAP)   Tel: (662) 288-1234
United Nations Building, Rajadamnern Nok Avenue   Fax: (662) 288-3022
Bangkok 10200, Thailand   Telex: 82392 ESCAP TH

READERSHIP SURVEY

The Macroeconomic Policy and Development Division of ESCAP is undertaking an evaluation of the publication *Asia-Pacific Development Journal*, with a view to improving the usefulness of future publications to our readers. We would appreciate it if you could complete this questionnaire and return it, at your earliest convenience, to:

Director
Macroeconomic Policy and Development Division
ESCAP, United Nations Building
Rajadamnern Nok Avenue
Bangkok 10200, THAILAND

QUESTIONNAIRE

	Excellent	Very good	Average	Poor
1. Please indicate your assessment of the *quality* of the publication in terms of:				
• presentation/format	4	3	2	1
• readability	4	3	2	1
• timeliness of information	4	3	2	1
• coverage of subject matter	4	3	2	1
• analytical rigour	4	3	2	1
• overall quality	4	3	2	1
2. How *useful* is the publication to your work?				
• provision of information	4	3	2	1
• clarification of issues	4	3	2	1
• its findings	4	3	2	1
• policy suggestions	4	3	2	1
• overall usefulness	4	3	2	1

3. Please give examples of how this publication has contributed to your work:

....

....

....

....

....

4.   Suggestions for improvement of similar publications:

....

....

....

....

5.   Your background information, please:

Name: ....

Title/position: ....

Institution: ....

Office address: ....

....

Please use additional sheets of paper, if required, to answer the questions.
Thank you for your kind cooperation in completing this questionnaire.

ASIA-PACIFIC DEVELOPMENT JOURNAL

INSTRUCTIONS TO CONTRIBUTORS

Published by the Macroeconomic Policy and Development Division (MPDD) of the United Nations Economic and Social Commission for Asia and the Pacific, the Asia-Pacific Development Journal provides a platform for the exchange of ideas and experiences on development issues and concerns facing the region and aims to stimulate policy debate and assist policy formulation. Published twice a year, the Journal welcomes policy-oriented articles and original pieces of work, focusing on development issues and challenges relevant to the Asian and the Pacific region.

1. MANUSCRIPTS

Authors are requested to provide copies of their manuscripts in English. The material should not have been previously published or submitted for publication elsewhere, and this should be stated by contributors in their covering letter to the Editorial Board. The manuscripts should be typed, double-spaced, on one side of white A4 paper and the length should not normally exceed 25-30 pages. Manuscripts are accepted subject to editorial revision.

Since all manuscripts will be refereed by professionals in the field, the name(s) of the author(s), institutional affiliation(s) and other identifying information should be placed on the title page only, in order to preserve anonymity. The title page should contain the following: (a) title; (b) name(s) of the author(s); (c) institutional affiliation(s); and (d) complete mailing address, telephone number, facsimile number and email address of the author, or of the primary author in the case of joint authors. The second page should contain the title, the name(s) of the author(s) and an abstract of approximately 150 words. Acknowledgements (if any) should appear after the abstract.

It is preferred that manuscripts be submitted by email to the address below (if hard copies are submitted, kindly provide two copies of the manuscript to the address below). The preferred word-processing software is MS Word. Once a manuscript is accepted for publication, the author(s) may be asked to submit electronic files of their manuscript, figures, tables and charts, as appropriate.

2. FOOTNOTES AND QUOTATIONS

Footnotes, if any, should be numbered consecutively with superscript Arabic numerals. They should be in double-spaced type. As the author-date system of referencing is to be used (see section 4 below), any footnotes should be of an explanatory nature. Quotations should be double-spaced. A copy of the page(s) of the original source of the quotation, as well as copy of the cover page of that source, should be provided.

3. TABLES AND FIGURES

All tables and figures should be numbered consecutively with Arabic numerals. Each table should be typed double-spaced. Tables and figures should be planned to fit the proportions of the printed page. Full source(s) should appear below the table/figure, followed by notes, if any, in lower-case letters.

4. REFERENCES

Authors should ensure that there is a complete reference for every citation in the text. References in the text should follow the author-date format, followed if necessary, by page numbers, for example, Becker (1964: 13-24). List only those references that are actually cited in the text or footnotes. References, listed alphabetically, should be typed double-spaced on a separate page in the following style:

Ahmed, E. and N. Stern (1983). "Effective taxes and tax reform in India", Discussion Paper 25, University of Warwick.

Desai, Padma, ed. (1883). Marxism, Central Planning, and the Soviet Economy (Cambridge, MA, MIT Press).

Krueger, Alan B. and Lawrence H. Summers (1987). "Reflections on the inter-industry wage structure", in Kevin Lang and Jonathan S. Leonard, eds., Unemployment and the Structure of Labour Markets (London, Basis Blackwell).

Sadorsky, P. (1994). "The behaviour of U.S. tariff rates: comment", American Economic Review, vol. 84, No. 4, September, pp. 1097-1103.

Terrones, M. (1987). "Macroeconomic policy cycle under alternative electoral structures: a signaling approach", unpublished.

For further details on referencing, please refer to the editorial guidelines at:
http://www.unescap.org/pdd/publications/questionnaire/apdj_editorial_guidelines.pdf.
The Editorial Board of the Asia-Pacific Development Journal wish to emphasize that papers need to be thoroughly edited in terms of the English language and authors are kindly requested to submit manuscripts that strictly conform to the editorial guidelines.

Manuscripts should be sent to:
Chief Editor, Asia-Pacific Development Journal
Macroeconomic Policy and Development Division
United Nations Economic and Social Commission for Asia and the Pacific
United Nations Building, Rajadamnern Nok Avenue, Bangkok 10200, Thailand.
Tel: (662) 288-1902; Fax: (662) 288-1000; (662) 288-3007; Email: escap-mpdd@un.org
Cable: ESCAP Bangkok